BEHIND THE FLIGHT DECK DOOR

INSIDER KNOWLEDGE ABOUT EVERYTHING
YOU'VE EVER WANTED TO ASK A PILOT

Brett Manders

PRAISE FOR *BEHIND THE FLIGHT DECK DOOR*

"I really enjoyed reading this as it is an easy read, and really relatable and quite entertaining. As a nervous flyer myself it was quite interesting and reassuring to read all the different things that go on behind the scenes and learn about the ins and outs of flying."
SARAH EMERSON
NERVOUS FLYER

"This book has so much valuable knowledge that every passenger wants to know and ask. So many things about aircraft, airlines and airports are such a mystery to many people, it is nice to have it explained is simple terms. After reading, I feel lots of little things that bothered me have been put in perspective and it has helped my fear of flying significantly. *Behind the Flight Deck Door* is a must have book for anyone who travels on airlines!"
NISHA SHARMA
NERVOUS FLYER

"I met Brett in the front galley one night flying back to Australia. He explained a great deal of things about why our flight was delayed and how they were trying to make up for the lost time. It was a great experience to actually speak face-to-face with a pilot, and a real thrill after landing to be invited into the cockpit so I could see what goes on "behind the flight deck door!"
This book will give you the same experience I had!"
ANDREW
PASSENGER

"Brett helped explain things to myself and my family when we were disrupted by the eruption of a volcano in Bali in late 2017. He explained things clearly and reassured us we would only fly if it was safe."
SALLY BINOTTO
PASSENGER

"I always wondered if it was possible to open a door mid-flight, and this book will definitely reassure that when the doors are closed, you are safe. I found it interesting the interface between the pilots and the computers and

who is controlling the plane. I would definitely recommend purchasing a copy to read on your flight."
RACHEL KATINIS
PASSENGER

"A really interesting book if you have ever been a passenger on a plane. I'd certainly recommend to other people to read."
LAURA SCARMOZZINO
PASSENGER

"Brett's uncomplicated, honest, and easy to understand book is a welcome addition on any flight. It offers an enlightening point of view of the all-important necessity of air travel with rare glimpses of the secret world airline pilots inhabit."
JULIE POSTANCE
AUTHOR, *BREAKING THE SOUND BARRIERS*

"An enthusiastic aviator, professional airline pilot and flight instructor, Brett is a young man passionate about his chosen career. As my own instructor, I have experienced first-hand his passion for teaching and the unique skill-set he possesses. However, it's not only his dedication to the professional role, but his genuine love of life and the stories and events he recalls that makes him truly unique."
SHAYNE GEORGE
B787 CAPTAIN
QANTAS

"I've been an international airline pilot for over 20 years. I have recently qualified to fly the new Boeing 787 Dreamliner and Brett was my instructor. Brett's instruction was excellent, and he delivered it with common-sense and humor. There is not much Brett doesn't know about what goes on behind the flight deck door."
C. TEALE
B787 FIRST OFFICER
QANTAS

"I had the pleasure of having Brett as my instructor for a large portion of my Boeing 787 endorsement.

Brett's enthusiasm for teaching meant that from day one, the correct procedures were followed. I can't thank him enough for this as laying the correct foundations at the beginning of anything new is paramount, especially when it comes to aviation.

The best thing about working with Brett was his teaching style. Brett always set a tone that was relaxed, friendly, and he always took the time to ensure I fully understood each and every procedure and the intent behind it. I admire people like Brett who have the ability of tapping into a student's 'way of thinking' in order to explain any subject matter – that, to me, is the definition of a great instructor.

Another aspect of Brett's teaching style that I highly admired was his ability to find a simple way of teaching a specific goal.

Brett is a highly-skilled, knowledgeable and professional pilot. He was most definitely an integral part of helping me successfully complete my endorsement."
TONY VAUGHAN
B787 FIRST OFFICER
JETSTAR AIRWAYS

"Mr. Manders was our instructor who taught us how to fly in 2003. His accurate demonstration of flying skills and strict standards set us up to be great pilots at the beginning of our careers.

He could always help us fix our mistakes but also helped build our confidence with each lesson.

He took the time to know about us and about our families. We have stayed in contact with him for over 10 years and hope to fly with him 'behind the flight deck door' again one day."
CAPTAIN LIAO WEI
CAPTAIN PENG XIANG
CAPTAIN CHEN QUILING
CHINA SOUTHERN AIRWAYS

Published in Australia by

Atlantis Media
Ivanhoe, Victoria 3079 Australia
Telephone: +61 407 566 514
Email: atlantismedia787@gmail.com
Website www.behindtheflightdeckdoor.com
Twitter: @flightdeckdoor
Instagram: @theflightdeckdoor
First published in Australia 2018
Copyright © Brett Manders 2018

All rights reserved. No part of this publication may be reproduced, stored in a retrieval system, or transmitted, in any form or by any means without the prior written permission of the publisher, nor be otherwise circulated in any form of binding or cover other than that in which it is published and without a similar condition being imposed on the subsequent purchaser.

A catalogue record for this book is available from the National Library of Australia

ISBN 978-0-6482356-0-6 Print
ISBN 978-0-6482356-1-3 Ebook

Cover photography by Vortex Aviation Photography
www.vortexaviationphotography.com.au

Cover layout and design by C7creativezone
email: zeeshanshamsupwork@gmail.com

Typesetting & Layout by Abbasi Ssemwanga
email: abby.sem07@gmail.com

Illustrations by www.paulcoxillustrations.com

Printed by Ingram Spark

Disclaimer

All care has been taken in the preparation of the information herein, but no responsibility can be accepted by the publisher or author for any damages resulting from the misinterpretation of this work. All contact details given in this book were current at the time of publication, but are subject to change. The advice given in this book is based on the experience of the individuals. Professionals should be consulted for individual problems. The author and publisher shall not be responsible for any person with regard to any loss or damage caused directly or indirectly by the information in this book.

ABOUT THE AUTHOR

Brett Manders is a pilot with an Australian Airline.

A former Naval Officer, he felt ships travelled too slowly, so turned his skills to flying. He has over 10,000 hours flying experience and has flown Airbus A320, A321, A330, and the Boeing B787 Dreamliner. He is completing a Bachelor of Aviation Management and currently conducts type-rating training on the B787 Simulator.

He has lived in Singapore and all over Australia, but currently calls Melbourne home. Brett lives with his wife, Kirsty, daughter Amara and his dog, Harvey. He still enjoys going to the airport even when on vacation, and still looks up to watch planes fly overhead. Brett is an avid reader who loves bike riding, the gym, and is a passionate supporter of the Richmond Football Club.

*Thanks Mum and Dad,
for the "stick with it" pep talks, because I got there in the end.*

CONTENTS

Welcome on board	xvi
Chapter 1 – Before Departure	**1**
Check-in	1
Flight planning	3
The flight plan	3
Weather	3
NOTAMS – Notice to Airmen/Airwomen	4
Volcanoes	5
Fuel	6
Security screening	7
Why does everybody have a laptop?	9
I have sped through security screening; how do I speed through immigration?	9
I am your nervous flyer	10
Aircraft checks	10
Engines turning while the aircraft is parked	12
The hard facts on commercial accidents?	12
Pilots and coffee	14
Pilots, alcohol, and drugs	14
Overbooking	15
Wing inspection markings	16
What is with the delays?	16
The barking dog noises	18
What about animals, how do they travel?	20
Do you transport bodies? What if somebody dies inflight?	21
Can I find out about my pilots before the flight?	21
Chapter 2 – During Flight	**23**
Checklists	23
Seatbelts	24
Turbulence	24
Jettison fuel/dump fuel	30
Wingtip vortices and chemtrails	30
Letters and numbers on the ground	31
Do you really fly it or is it the autopilot?	33

Bad weather	36
What if we get hit by lightning?	37
Can pilots fly different aircraft types?	38
Radios and losing radio contact	39
What call signs do they give you?	40
Alpha Bravo Charlie Zulu and the phonetics	40
What happens if you hit a bird?	41
Are aircraft germ labs?	43
Can you get sucked in or stuck on a toilet seat?	44
Does the toilet flush out into the air?	44
Is it possible for somebody to open a door in flight?	45
How do you open doors in an emergency?	46
Reclining Seats	47
Air rage and air frustrations	48
I saw my pilot in the galley. Who is flying?	51
Smoking in a plane	52
What is a knot?	52
How does a jet engine work?	53
What does final approach mean?	53
Speed restrictions. Are there speed cameras?	54
If pilots can speed up after delays, why don't you fly faster all the time?	55
Air routes and short cuts	56
Ice on the wings	57

Chapter 3 – After Landing — 61

The difference between good landings and a bad one	61
Domestic vs international	61
Do you want to fly the big ones?	62
Are you a Captain? What are the other pilots called?	64
What is seniority and is there really a seniority list?	64
Can you visit the cockpit?	65
What are the ongoing requirements and training?	66
How do you beat jetlag?	67

Chapter 4 – I Hate It When — 69

I hear we have a slight technical delay	69
We are just waiting on the last of the paperwork	70
- The aircraft's technical or tech log.	71
- Fuel receipts and dockets.	71
- Load and balance paperwork.	72
Delays and the nervous flyer	74
Tray table, seat back, and window shade	75
Lights dimmed in the cabin	76

Chapter 5 – Uniform — **79**
Hats — 79
Sunglasses — 79
Short Sleeves — 79
Epaulettes — 81
Ties — 81
Wings — 82
Nav bags — 82

Chapter 6 – What Can I See? — **85**
All the colored lights on an aircraft mean? — 85
Navigation — 85
Rotating beacon — 86
Anti-Collison lights — 86
Landing — 86
Taxy — 86
Runway turn off — 86
Four-engine planes have to be better than two-engine — 87
Could I be talked through a landing? — 88
How does a plane actually fly?? — 88
What is a stall? — 91
Can we glide? — 91
Why do you take off into wind? — 92

Chapter 7 – Aircraft Equipment — **93**
Handcuffs – yes — 93
Sky Marshals — 93
Crash axe — 94
Fire extinguishers — 94
Crew rest compartments — 94
Defibrillator — 95
Portable Oxygen — 95
Surveillance cameras — 96
Grab Handles — 96
Cockpit camera — 97

Chapter 8 – Miscellaneous — **99**
Future Technology — 99
Pilotless aircraft — 100
Pilot error — 102
MH370, will they find it? — 102
In light of an accident — 103
Who is the safest/best airline? — 104

What about low-cost carriers? Are they still safe?	104
Is a Boeing safer than an Airbus?	104
Can girls be pilots?	105

Chapter 9 – The Two Most Popular Questions — 107
How much money do you earn? — 107
Do you get free flights? — 107

In conclusion — 109
Interviews — 111
Glossary — 115
With thanks — 119

WELCOME ON BOARD

Ladies and gentlemen, welcome on board. We will be underway shortly on your journey to understanding all the secrets held behind the flight deck door.

We are expecting smooth reading conditions on today's flight and predict you will be thoroughly impressed with the service, and all you will learn.

We are just completing the last of the book's paperwork, and I will speak to you again before we reach our destination. So sit back, relax, and enjoy the read.

This book is born out of all questions I have been asked when people discover I am a pilot. I can't make you a professional pilot, but I can put you on the right path to understand what is going on at any given time.

All these little bits of wisdom will see you become a savvy traveler. For when your fellow travelers ask the questions, you will have the answers!

This is not a technical book. It is written in simple and plain language to convey as much information to you as I can.

Since the horrible events of 9/11, flight decks of modern airliners have become somewhat of an enigma. I remember as a young child and then as a student pilot asking to go up into the cockpit to have a look around and talk to the pilots.

Unfortunately, that is now a bygone era and the only opportunity most people would get to visit would be at the end of a flight. By that stage, most people just want to get off the plane. This is a shame as most pilots are more than happy to show you 'the office.'

More and more people are taking to the skies every day for work or for leisure, and whilst many simply endure the things they hate about flying, most still find the industry somewhat fascinating.

So what really goes on behind the bullet-proof door? And what does the pilot mean when he or she says...

CHAPTER 1

BEFORE DEPARTURE

CHECK-IN

So, you are checking in. Or, maybe you have checked in online or on your smart phone and are dropping your bag off. Depending on the time you arrive, your pilots may also be checking in their luggage. If you hate queuing, then checking in online will minimize your wait time. Usually the queue for bag drop is shorter and moves quicker.

This, of course, will depend on whether the pilots have a scheduled overnight, i.e. staying away from home-base. Again, this depends on the aircraft size, length of the flight, and the airline itself. Low-cost carriers save money by returning crew to their home-base at the end of a shift. It saves on the costs associated with crews overnighting (transport, accommodation and meal allowances).

This, in turn, reduces airline costs and, accordingly, fares should be cheaper. The downside of not having crews overnight is that the first flight of the day – often required by business travelers – is later, as the aircraft may have to fly in from somewhere else first.

Your pilots have checked in at the same check-in desks as you. However, they still have their black 'Nav bags' in tow as they walk off to 'sign on.' What is in these mystery bags? I will leave that to the section on uniform, as it is really exciting... Well, maybe not, but I would like you to keep reading!

We have all checked in, and our bags have disappeared below into the depths of the unseen part of the airport to be sorted and loaded onto the flight. This is the time you have probably gone for a coffee, browsed the shops, and hopefully bought this book!

The pilots are now signing on in a crew room. With the advent of modern technology, that is changing. It is possible that crews may sign on remotely using tablets etc. Sign on lets the company know we are at work. Anybody can be late; you could sleep in, hit a traffic jam, forget your identification or passport. But when it happens to the pilots, the company needs to know so they can keep the operation running smoothly and on time.

Case Study:

An 'Ohnosecond' is the time it takes to realize you have left something important behind.

I drove to work once and forgot my company identification. It allows me to access parking and briefing rooms. As I was about to enter the car park, I reached for my ID then said, "oh no." It was still on the kitchen bench.

Fortunately, I lived close by and had left in plenty of time to turn around and go back to collect it. I rang crewing to let them know I might be late, but I was on my way. I also rang my wife to have the ID ready to throw through the car window as I passed by home.

Sounds like a pain and yes, it is. However, often times it can be worse coming home. A few pilots will, after clearing Immigration, place their passports in their shirt-top pockets. You can imagine, coming home tired and getting out of your work clothes, maybe not concentrating, or somebody else picks up the clothes to put in the wash.

You can see where this is going right? It turns into quite an expensive exercise. Passports take time to produce. When you may need it in a few days for work it becomes an issue when your current one is slightly water logged! You can get a replacement created express-style, but you pay for the privilege.

Learn from an expert – as soon as you have finished with your passport, put it in a secure travel wallet!

At sign on we are also receiving details of anything new we need to know. Each company will have its own names for these things, but they can entail changes to company or manufacturers procedures, or just simple notices. We confirm receipt of the information, and that we understand their content. However, most pilots would check this information on tablets and smart phones well beforehand. It may be even looked at out of work hours. We do this earlier to ensure we understand it, and mostly to save precious time.

FLIGHT PLANNING

In years gone by, we would then start printing a 'flight-planning package.' This package is made up of a number of parts including: the flight plan itself, weather, Notices to Airmen/women, volcanoes, and fuel.

THE FLIGHT PLAN

Aircraft fly to designated waypoints along air corridors or routes. These are like roads in the sky. These routes assist air traffic controllers to provide spacing between aircraft. However, unlike your car, we can maneuver off these routes if required – to avoid bad weather, for instance. We cannot merely decide to go off the cleared route. If every aircraft did that, it would be chaos and separation between aircraft would reduce to unacceptable levels. We have to ask for and receive a clearance to deviate from our cleared route from an air traffic controller.

The flight plan has a lot of information that needs to be digested: the flight time length, which route we are flying to our destination (it can differ due to head or tail winds, weather, airspace closures due to military exercises etc.,), and our expected time of arrival at various waypoints.

WEATHER

Weather will be looked at next. Not only for our departure but also for our destination and any en-route airports we may like to consider for emergency-planning purposes. We will also look at upper-level wind forecasts to see if any turbulence is possible. Often a graphic will be presented in order to aid in the quick digestion of this information – a picture tells a thousand words!
A forecast for an airport might look like this:

WSSS 260850Z 2609/2712 14009KT 9999 FEW018CB SCT020
PROB30 TEMPO 2609/2612 3000 TSRA FEW012CB BKN015
TEMPO 2703/2706 5000 SHRA BKN025

It might appear confusing, but it is all abbreviations and times. This is a forecast from Singapore that was issued on the 26th day of the month at 0850Z. This time and the time stamp 'Z' refers to Greenwich Mean Time (GMT). All times in aviation work in one time zone, as it makes it easier for crews to work in one time zone.

NOTAMS – NOTICE TO AIRMEN/AIRWOMEN

Pilots also look at things called NOTAMs. This is an abbreviation of Notices to Airman. They give all manner of information that may prevent your flight from being conducted. We look for big things, like runways or taxiways being closed for inspections or cleaning. With each landing, aircraft leave a bit of rubber on the road. This reduces water run-off if it rains and may decrease braking effectiveness, so regular steam cleaning of the runways is required to blast this rubber clear. Also, navigation aids can be turned off for testing or maintenance. There could be a crane near a runway and it may impinge on 'the safe area.' Passenger transport aircraft have to be able to perform to a certain level and climb at prescribed rates even after an engine failure. (If you are a nervous flyer reading this, yes, I have mentioned the unmentionable, but I will explain in a little more detail further on, and that will hopefully allay your

Case Study:
Get your words planned before you speak on the P.A.

When I was a fresh-faced airline pilot, I was keen to complete the P.A. I committed the cardinal sin of not thinking about time zones before I pressed the button to speak. It is an awful feeling to say, "and we are going to arrive at ..." and your mind goes blank. I can think on my feet quickly, and apologized for an Air Traffic Control interruption. I learnt my lesson and always write notes before I start to talk.

I have also heard other crews announce a flight to a different destination than to where the plane is actually going. That certainly gets everybody in the passenger cabin listening! It is quickly followed up by an amended announcement.

I have also sat next to a crew-member making an announcement, and this particular pilot forgot my name. I could have helped out and spoken it or shown my ID. But it was more fun to laugh at his predicament when I covered up my ID.

These mishaps can occur due to crews just forgetting, being tired, or minds thinking of the next sector.

---

fears.) There can't be any obstacles within a certain area or splay. In the case of the crane, performance of the aircraft would have to be adjusted to ensure it remains clear of objects.

NOTAMs may also inform you about hazards. Birds and bats are two big ones that seem to frequent airport environments. There isn't a lot you can do about them, but it just helps your awareness of what to expect.

VOLCANOES

Pilots will also look to see if there are any Volcanic Ash advisories. Volcanic Ash is really bad for aircraft. Radar cannot pick it up and at night you can't see it. If an aircraft flies through it, chances are the engines will stop running. It happened to a British Airways Boeing 747 in 1982, which had all four of its engines fail. The ash is also very abrasive, so the pilots may not be able to see out of the windows for landing if they are scratched up.

The world is divided into nine areas called VAACs – Volcanic Ash Advisory Centers. Each VAAC researches and analyzes the actual and impending volcanic eruptions. The sections are based in:
Anchorage, United States
Buenos Aires, Argentina
Darwin, Australia
London, United Kingdom
Montreal, Canada
Tokyo, Japan
Toulouse, France
Washington, United States
Wellington, New Zealand

Rest assured, airlines and pilots are very risk averse and will avoid these areas by a long way. As a side note, pilots practice inadvertently flying into volcanic ash in simulator training sessions. This is to ensure we can practice the procedures we need should the situation arise. Firstly, leave the area of the ash quickly and if the engine(s) do fail, to get them running again quickly. See the section on ongoing requirements.

FUEL
After the flight plan, and weather and NOTAM information has been digested, the crew members will then look at the fuel plan.

The flight fuel is calculated on flying from point A to point B at a given altitude and weight. Then there is extra added for taxi, flying to an alternate airport, variable reserve, fixed reserve, maneuvering fuel, and weather/traffic contingency.

Taxi fuel is generally a fixed number - usually a few hundred kilos depending upon the size of the aircraft. Think of that next time you are filling up the family car at the gas station!

Contingency fuel allows for delays due to weather and traffic. At busy airports, often a certain amount of traffic holding will be added as a NOTAM. For example, Sydney airport has a curfew and a lot of aircraft will arrive just as the airport is opening. To avoid the possibility of an aircraft needing to declare a fuel emergency, there will be a NOTAM saying that should you arrive within this period, you must have a certain amount of minutes of traffic-holding fuel.

If there are thunderstorms forecast, aircraft must have holding fuel to allow them to hold until the storms clear. Thunderstorms are often forecast as periods of INTER (30 minutes) or TEMPO (60 minutes). If the storms do not have these timeframes, an aircraft may have to carry sufficient fuel to divert to an alternate airport.

There can be other weather forecasts such as fog, that may require an aircraft to have fuel to hold or divert to another airport.

Reserve fuel has two components: variable and fixed. It is company and regulating authority dependent. Some generic examples would be:

Variable reserve can be 10% of the flight fuel up to a certain limit. This allows for un-forecast headwinds and/or delays en route. It is ok if this fuel is consumed.

Fixed reserved is calculated at 30 minutes of fuel at a low altitude. A jet engine uses significantly more fuel at low level than it does at cruise. This fuel must be in the tanks at completion of the landing roll. If this fuel is used in flight, a fuel emergency must be declared. This is hoped to prevent an aircraft suffering from a fuel exhaustion event. By declaring a fuel emergency, ATC will prioritize that aircraft for landing.

These fuel figures are presented in the flight planning package for the crew. They will then discuss any other contingencies that may arise. This could include things such as a long taxi time or the possibility of being held down and not reaching the planned level straight away. If you are down lower, you burn more fuel. The crew will then discuss if any extra fuel (called discretionary fuel uplift) is to be added. The Captain has absolute authority to uplift more. However, the Captain is also cognizant that any extra fuel is extra weight that must be carried and will, in turn, affect the fuel burn. On a medium-range flight of eight hours, an extra thousand pounds (or kilos) of fuel may burn an extra 150 pounds (or kilos) of fuel just to carry it. So, if an extra ton is required the crew will need to carry 1.2 tons to allow for the extra burn.

I HATE GOING THROUGH SECURITY SCREENING

Yes, me too! Every time I go to work. Most places are really good when it comes to security screening, while some airports are not so. What can make it more frustrating is the differences. Each country, and even airports in the same country, can have different restrictions. In Japan, the staff are fantastic. So friendly and courteous, but that is their culture. If you travel with young kids, head for Thailand. The Thai people love children, and if they see you are stressed-out parents of young kids, they will zoom you up to the front of the queue. Khob khun krup! (That means 'thank you' in Thai!)

Generally, passengers are happy with aircrew jumping to the head of the line ... after all, we could be flying your plane.

One good bit of advice I will give you is when you pick the security lane you are going to enter, choose carefully. Study the numbers or people and the types of travelers as you approach the lines.

There might be 5-10 business people in one line and some older folks or parents with young babies/children. Go behind the business travelers. They are probably regular travelers so will be quick and efficient when moving through the screening stations.

Chances are however, that you will get stuck behind the retirees who have all the time in the world. Or worse still, behind the parents who have to wake a sleeping baby, take the baby out of a pram, put the pram and all manner of stuff that infants need through the scanners. I know, I have been there myself. Something will inevitably be forgotten, which will set off the metal detector. The helpful security may offer to hold the child whilst the parent goes back through the scanner. The previously calm baby will launch into a scream that will resemble an air raid siren. And I am not picking on parents of small children. On this one, I am truly speaking from experience.

Sorry to the old folks. My parents are recently retired, and I can see them forgetting to either take things like aerosols or laptops out of their bags. But time is more friendly, I guess, when you are retired. So they don't seem to rush as much!

SO WHY DOES EVERYBODY IN FRONT OF ME HAVE A LAPTOP THAT HAS TO BE REMOVED?

Well I can't claim to know why all the people in front of you do. Probably a bit of Murphy's Law going on? As to why they have to take them out, it is because a lap top is sufficiently dense enough that it prevents the x-ray from seeing through them. Thus, they could be used to conceal other items that are not permitted. It could be used to conceal a weapon, drugs, or animals.

By taking the laptop out it can be viewed as a standalone item. Is it a bit of overkill? Maybe, but security checks are designed to keep us safe. Whilst robust measures can be onerous, it is unlikely this will change any time soon. In fact, in 2017, the United States Department of Transport was contemplating banning laptops as carry-on luggage on some flights.

I HAVE SPED THROUGH SECURITY SCREENING; HOW DO I SPEED THROUGH IMMIGRATION?

There are a number of things you can do to ease your own burden of being processed through immigration quickly. Firstly, treat your passport like it is cash, gold, your cell phone, tablet, or other worldly good you possess. The number of people who lose passports is amazing. I have had passengers on board who have left theirs at duty-free counters, restaurants, boarding lounges and bars. It even happens at the destination, with some passengers leaving the aircraft without it.

Then there are those travelers who allow their passports to get wet. It might not necessarily be the full immersion in the washing machine, but merely having your passport close to your body in humid climates can allow moisture to penetrate. With more digital technology going into passports, this is not a good idea for the longevity of your passport.

Some other things you may not know about your ticket to travel the world:
- ✈ It is a crime to willfully damage your passport
- ✈ Take care of the photo page as even minor damage will prevent machine reading
- ✈ Don't use your passport as a surface to fill out documentation. It can leave marks and indentations, again preventing machine reading
- ✈ If your passport fills up but is still valid, you need another one.
- ✈ Keep your passport in a travel wallet to prevent it getting bent, wet, or misplaced.

While you are waiting in the queue have your passport and documents ready. Listen to what is asked of those passengers ahead of you so you can fly through immigration.

Finally, a smile and polite conversation with the custom/immigration/boarder protection staff can certainly do no harm.

I AM A NERVOUS FLYER. I DON'T WANT TO CRASH. HOW DO I KNOW IT WON'T HAPPEN?

Being afraid of flying is quite common. It is not unusual to have a minor delay and people who are concerned will offload themselves. They imagine all manner of disaster scenarios.

If you are a nervous flyer, I can understand and empathize. Not afraid of flying? You can skip this section but you may be sitting next to somebody who has fears and you can help to allay those, and increase your kudos as a savvy traveler.

You may have been told that your fears are objectively irrational. Internally you are reacting rationally to flying as you see it. You have seen the news with airline crashes and you believe somehow the plane you are on is going to crash.

It is the perception that is held that is skewed, not the reaction to the perception. I am not (and if you are trying to convince a fearful flyer) going to tell you that you are wrong, explain hard facts or punish you for your beliefs. That will not help a person to change their feelings.

What must be done is empathetically enquire as to why they feel that way. Has there been a traumatic experience or a fact misinterpretation? Once the reasoning can be uncovered, the reaction can hopefully be modified.

AIRCRAFT CHECKS

One thing I will often mention is an airliner is checked thoroughly. It is checked at the start of the day, the end of the day, before it does long over-water flights, and on each turn-around. A turn-around is when the aircraft completes a flight and the same crew continues on to do another sector.

During these checks all the safety-related systems are checked to be in working order. The pilots and engineers also do a walk around to confirm everything 'looks' ok. You may enquire if they did that to the car they travelled in to the airport?

"But hang on. I have watched that television show, *Air Crash Investigation*," I hear you say.

How many series are they up to now? They must keep crashing if they keep making new episodes.

Unfortunately, when an airplane crashes, it is often spectacular, and loss of life can be high. It is headline-grabbing, and fodder for the media. There is an old news maxim, 'if it bleeds, it leads.'

Loss of life makes headlines. The media also use emotive language. As I write this in October 2017, there was a report of an aircraft that fell 20,000 feet when the cabin lost pressurization. The aircraft didn't fall or plunge, it was flown down to a safe altitude as fast as possible whilst under the control of the pilots. The media sensationalizes what is a proper response to a non-normal condition.

So, you are a nervous flyer and here in the very next sentence I have written the magical thing that will make everything ok and forget your fear of flying. Sorry, but that isn't the case. Yes, airliners have crashed, and though I wish it wasn't the case, they will crash again.

So, how on Earth do people front up and go flying. Air Transport is one of the safest modes of transport available. Trains derail, ships sink, and I won't mention the number of people who are killed in road accidents annually.

The fear you have of crashing is rational. However, the chances of it happening are remote in the extreme. But what about those air crash investigation television shows? The reason they can actually be produced is there is so much data available to analyze after the event. The maintenance records are extremely thorough. You can pick up a maintenance log and see if light bulbs or tires were changed, if an aircraft has had any work done to it. It is, to put it simply, the life story of the plane that is held on the aircraft, and a back-up copy is available to investigators should it be required.

With all this information available, it allows the books and television show – *Air Craft Investigation* - to be produced. Is it macabre? Possibly. However, all previous accidents have, in some way, made flying even safer. With each event, there are lessons learnt for engineering, pilots, air traffic controllers, airliner operators, and regulating authorities.

These lessons translate into changes to the way things are done. It could mean change to aircraft equipment, standard operating procedures, or rules - depending upon the outcome of the investigations.

So, is it ok to be nervous? Sure it is. But for each crash or accident that springs to your mind, there is some outcome that has made the aircraft you are on now, safer.

WHY ARE THE ENGINES TURNING WHILE THE AIRCRAFT IS PARKED?

The engines are not running. Fuel is expensive. Probably the biggest expenditure any airline has. The engines are started during 'push back', and shut down as soon as the aircraft has parked.

There is very little internal resistance within the core of a jet engine. This is partly why they are so fuel efficient. So it only takes a little breeze and the front part of the engine or fan will rotate. It even happens if the wind is coming from behind the aircraft.

You can tell if the engines are running as the rotating/flashing red beacon on the aircraft will be on.

OK, I AM NOT A NERVOUS FLYER. WHAT ARE THE HARD FACTS ON COMMERCIAL ACCIDENTS?

The Aviation Safety Network (https://aviation-safety.net) is a great website with a wealth of safety-related (and yes accident-related) data. Even with all that data, there are a myriad of different ways I could present the answers.

In 2016 there were approximately 35 million commercial airline flights. There was a total of 19 fatal accidents resulting in 325 fatalities. Of those fatalities, 195 occurred in Pakistan, Colombia, or Russia. There were only six accidents where more than 10 people were killed. Two accidents were planes operated by airlines on the European Union's blacklist. That means they don't meet required safety standards to operate in European airspace.

How does that look in terms of percentage? Infinitesimally small. Given the approximate worldwide air traffic of about 35,000,000 flights, the accident rate is one fatal passenger flight accident in every 3,200,000 flights.

The Aviation Safety Network website quotes ASN President Harro Ranter: "Since 1997 the average number of airliner accidents has shown a steady and persistent decline, for a great deal thanks to the continuing safety-driven efforts by international aviation organizations such as ICAO, IATA, Flight Safety Foundation and the aviation industry."

The year 2016 was one of the safest years in air safety on record and it is continually improving every year. See graphic below.

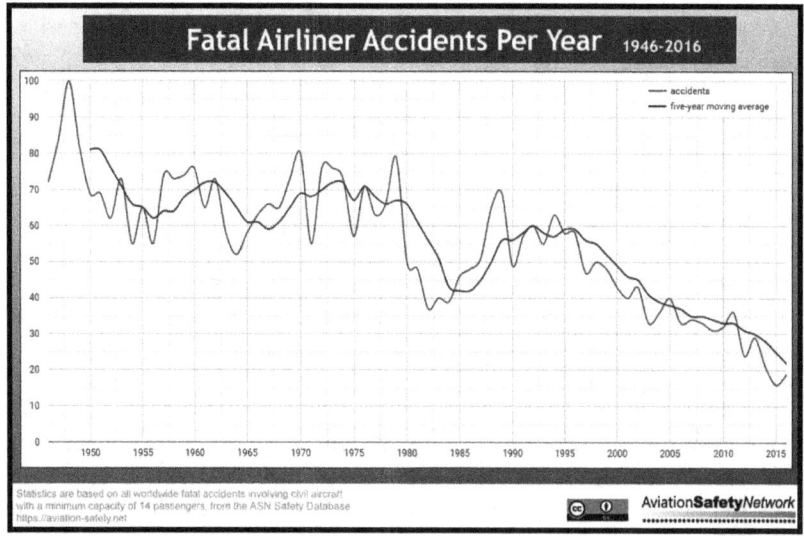

(Source: www.https://aviation-safety.net)

Don't forget, the pilots and cabin crew all have family and friends who want us home safely too. We have a vested interest in getting you safely to your destination.

I think that on some level, most people have a part of them that is afraid to fly. Yes, even your author has not so much a fear of flying, rather a healthy respect for what I do and the outcomes of my actions.

Today, there is so much more knowledge, technology and training that goes a long way to improving safety. ICAO (International Civil Aviation Organization) has tasked airlines to embrace programs called SMS (Safety Management Systems). An SMS is a systematic approach to managing safety, including the organizational structures needed, who is accountable, the policies and procedures. It operates under the theory 'if you can measure it, you can manage it.'

In this case, what is safety? How do you do safety well? And how do you measure safety?

Safety is the state in which the possibility of harm to persons or damage to property is reduced to, and maintained at or below, an acceptable level. This is achieved by a continual process of hazard identification and risk management.

Obviously, the complete removal of aircraft accidents and/or serious incidents remains the fundamental aim. Aviation will never be completely free of hazards and risks. Human beings and the systems we build cannot be certain to be free from mistakes and their consequences. The only way, thus far, to never have accidents is to never fly. What we seek to achieve is the appropriate balance that ensures the protection of safety of aviation and the production of flying you from point A to B.

An airline's SMS is made up of four areas: Policy and Objectives, Risk Management, Assurance and Promotion, and Training. It is really trying to pre-empt safety related issues before they occur, rather than the old way of analyze accident data after the fact.

For example, my airline has a self-reporting program where anybody can self-report if you make a mistake. If you do this, you are not punished. The data you provide is de-identified, collated, and analyzed by airlines and safety regulators to see if a trend is occurring. Either the airline or the regulator can take preemptive actions to prevent worse things occurring.

DO PILOTS AND COFFEE GO HAND IN HAND?

Pretty much. Much better to have a proper coffee before being subjected to the aircraft supply! Not every pilot drinks it but I know it has certainly become a habit for me. We may be starting work at any time of the day or night. If I have a proper espresso coffee it makes me feel like I have reset my body clock and am saying to myself, 'right we have a long day/night ahead of us and we are just starting.'

CAN PILOTS DRINK ALCOHOL? WHAT ABOUT DRUGS?

For legal purposes, 0.02% is the maximum blood alcohol concentration allowable for flight crew. In Australia, Civil Aviation Regulation (CAR) 256 controls the timing of alcohol ingestion for people who operate in safety sensitive areas.

The legal wording states: 'A person shall not act as, or perform any duties or functions preparatory to acting as, a member of the operating crew of an aircraft if the person has during the period of 8 hours immediately preceding the departure of the aircraft consumed any alcoholic liquor.'

A much simpler way pilots refer to this is the 8-hour bottle to throttle rule. Under this regulation, the following are strict liability offences and don't refer to any specific blood-alcohol concentration percentages. There is some ambiguity when relating to a person acting as a crew, is impaired; entering an aircraft while in a state of intoxication or be operating an aircraft where impairment due to ingestion of alcohol or consume alcohol on board.

Pilots, therefore, must be aware that any level of intoxication could be enough to result in prosecution or other disciplinary measures in addition to employment consequences. In doesn't matter if it has been 12 hours since drinking that you are signing on. Most pilots err on the side of extreme caution, knowing their own tolerances for alcohol and their body's reactions to its consumption. It is most surely not like the 2012 Denzel Washington movie, *Flight*, where he was drinking and taking drugs whilst on the job!

It is nice to enjoy a drink after a day (or night's) work, but pilots are cognizant that they can be breath tested at work by your employer and/or the safety regulator. I have been breath tested for alcohol and drug tested in crew rooms, aerobridges and even in the cockpit. I don't, and I am sure most pilots don't mind. We know the rules and have worked hard to earn our licenses. There is too much at risk to throw it away on a big night, and I could think of nothing worse than being hungover on an aircraft!

OVERBOOKING

This is an airline practice to ensure they have the minimum number of vacant seats. If a retail shop fails to sell an item, no problem. They can sell it tomorrow. The problem with airline seats is, once that flight departs, they can never sell it again. Airlines have mountains of statistical data on the number of people who don't show up to their flight for various reasons. There are probably algorithms relating to price of the ticket, time of day, etc.

Years ago, airlines were granted approval to overbook, or sell more tickets than were seats available. This allows them to get more revenue and thereby offer cheaper seats to the travelling public.

Unfortunately, overbooking seats has recently made the news for all the wrong reasons. In the United States in early 2017, law enforcement officials dragged a passenger off an overbooked flight. It sometimes happens that everybody who has booked turns up and there are more people than seats available.

This is where the gate or ground staff will try to entice passengers to give up their spot for some kind of benefit. Maybe they will upgrade you to business class on the next flight or give you vouchers or discounts. In this case, nobody volunteered to get off, so the airline chose a passenger and he was quite rightly not happy about it. Unfortunately, all this stuff is written into the terms and agreements that you click on before you confirm your purchase. You read those terms and conditions, right?

Is it right that they do this? Well, I think everybody would prefer to have cheaper airfares on the small chance this could happen. If you think about other industries, they do likewise. Doctors are notorious for overbooking to ensure a steady supply of patients, but it is the patients who wait. Delivery drivers and tradesmen, too, will take on more work to ensure a continual flow of business.

WHAT IS THE LITTLE BLACK TRIANGLE STICKER INSIDE THE CABIN WALL OF AN AIRBUS AIRCRAFT MEAN?

If you stand at one end of the aircraft and look down all the rows. It all kind of looks the same. Same for the aircrew. If we need to inspect something outside on the wing, it is an easy reference for crew to walk to. As I typed this out, I pointed them out to my wife and she had never noticed them before. Most people don't, but hey that's what this book is all about.

It may be disconcerting for a passenger to see a pilot walk down and appear to look out multiple windows trying to find which window to view the wing. By having that little reference mark, we can confidently walk to the exact point we need to look out in the correct spot.

Why would we have to look at the wing? There could be a number of reasons, such as checking there is no ice on the upper surface. Ice disrupts the smooth flow of air over the upper surface of the wing. If you have disrupted airflow, the aircraft can stall or not produce enough lift for take-off.

There could also be a bird strike or abnormal engine indications in the cockpit. Sometimes a visual inspection can give us further information or peace of mind that everything is ok.

WHAT IS WITH THE DELAYS?

Each airline, each pilot, and probably each ground or gate staff member has their own way of describing a delay. It could be technical, operational, crewing, weather, Air Traffic Control, or waiting for connecting passengers.

I discuss the technical delay in the section: 'I hate it when…' I am sure most delays could be lumped into this category, but I will give you a little background on each.

Operational: sometimes busy airports can be constrained by the amount of arrivals and departures they can process. Ngurah Rai airport in Bali is one, as it is has a single runway with not a lot of parking bays to accommodate all the airlines and aircraft that want to fly in. All the world's busy airports have a similar system.

In these instances, the aerodrome operator allocates slots that are like bookings. These are a window of opportunity the aircraft must use to arrive or depart. Miss your slot for any reason, the pilots will have to contact the airline's operational control who will liaise with the airport operator to get a new slot.

Crewing: on some occasions, crew 'run out of hours.' Pilots and cabin crew have very specific limits on the number of hours we are allowed to work. Whilst pilots have been called glorified bus drivers, and people think cabin crew are airborne waiters/waitresses, we actually have roles related to safety. You don't want your crew suffering from fatigue should an emergency happen.

It may have transpired that something, often other delays, have caused one or more of the crew to be unable to complete their flight. This will mean the crewing department will have to contact somebody else to come and complete the duty.

Sometimes this crew member might be at the airport, or they could be on 'standby or available.' This duty means you are at the airline's disposal to cover flights if somebody gets sick or cannot complete a duty. We have to be ready to go, but they do allow a certain amount of time to get to the airport.

Crewing departments watch these limits pretty closely and will call people in advance. However, the problem presents itself if this advance call doesn't happen, or it takes time for the crew to get to the airport.

So, if you do hear of a crewing delay, rest assured your crew are just as concerned about the delay, and will do all they can to get you back on schedule.

Weather: possibly the easy one to explain. Thunderstorms in and around an airport really put the brakes on operations. Pilots don't want to fly near them and depending on local regulations, ramp staff may not be allowed on the tarmac when storms are within a certain distance.

An airport could have multiple runways, but due to strong winds only one is open for take-offs and landings. This will slow down departures and arrivals. It will also cause consequential delays down the line for airports that aren't affected by the weather system.

So, you can see working in the operations or crewing departments of an airline is like playing chess, except the board keeps moving!

Case Study:
Keep the passengers informed.

After several delays, some crewmembers were about to run out of duty time but opted to extend their duty. This is akin to agreeing to do overtime. They agreed, as they wanted to ensure the passengers made it to their destination.

Passengers can get annoyed if there is no information about the reason for and the likely duration of the delay. Cabin crew often bear the brunt of this frustration.

The Captain went out into the cabin and made an address over the P.A. facing everybody. He explained the cause of the ongoing delays and stressed it was not the cabin crew's fault. By extending their duty they were ensuring you arrived at your destination. His exact words following that were: "if you want to throw rotten tomatoes or angry words, come and throw them at me."

We never had any dramas. We know information is the key. People can handle the delays, it is the uncertainty that gets people frustrated.

Connecting passengers: depending on how tickets are sold, or passengers have planned their journeys, there can be connecting passengers. The airline doesn't like to fly with empty seats so depending on a number of factors, they will wait. It may be domestic passengers with an international connection or vice versa. If you were running late for your flight, due to circumstances beyond your control, you would like it if the pilots waited. We can catch up some delays in the air. We just have to pedal harder to go faster!

WHAT IS THE BARKING DOG NOISE YOU HEAR WHEN THE AIRCRAFT IS PUSHING BACK FROM THE GATE?

No, it is not canines in distress in the cargo hold. You may have never heard it yourself, but you will the next time you are on an Airbus narrow-body aircraft. By that I mean the A319, A320, A321 family.

It's a muffled sound, but sufficiently loud enough for passengers to hear. It can be a droning sound, a high-pitched humming, or more often than not, a woof-woof sound.

Case Study:
How can wind delay the plane?

One day there was a very strong northerly wind and only the north-south runway was in operation. Due to works on some of the taxiways, there was only one taxiway open to this particular runway.

This was in the early-morning peak hour traffic. There were plenty of jets taxiing to depart. It was, however, a slow process as the departures had to be spaced between the arriving aircraft.

Unfortunately, my aircraft had been down in the maintenance area. It needed to be towed back against the flow of departing aircraft.

Air Traffic Control couldn't delay other aircraft to tow ours against the flow. We just had to wait and take the delay on the chin. Being in the boarding gate allowed us to explain to the passengers what the reason for the delay was.

Just to add another twist to this story. We were flying to Singapore and we had to arrive before a certain time as the airspace around Changi Airport was going to be closed for their National Day celebrations.

We had to fly faster to make up for the delay. This uses more fuel and costs more. You can see why airlines hate delays too!

It is completely normal even though it does resemble an engine trying to start over and over again, and not succeeding. Passengers will often mention it to cabin crew. They may bring it to our attention, or not if they are used to the noise themselves. Often though, cabin crew can't give the factual explanation, which is ok as they know it is a normal sound. Sometimes, the cabin crew mention it to us, and if I have time I will go down and reassure the passengers that all is ok and provide the following information.

The Airbus aircraft have a number of hydraulic systems on board. They are powered by their respective engine. The green system is pressurized by engine 1 on the left, and the yellow system is pressurized by engine 2 on the right. Left and right is different depending on which way you are looking at the aircraft. By convention we refer to numbers/sides as if you are looking to the front of the aircraft (or sitting in your forward-facing seat).

Also, by convention, all the equipment (aerobridges, stairs, ground power and air) is located on the left-hand side of the aircraft, probably because that is the side the Captain sits. The right-hand engine is normally (but not always) started first. In order to save time and precious fuel, we don't want to have both engines running before we start pushing back. The right-hand side is usually clear of any obstructions first. The loading staff will already be working on the next aircraft. But to do so we require steering. The steering is powered by the green hydraulic systems on the left-hand side of the plane.

This is where a nifty piece of equipment called a PTU (power transfer unit) starts to work. It enables the yellow system to power the green system, and vice versa. It automatically activates whenever the difference between the two systems is greater than 500PSI. They normally operate at about 2500psi, but some aircraft operate at 5000psi. As the pressure drops, the PTU cycles on and off and pressurizes the green system so nose-wheel steering is available. It can also activate during periods of high demand, such as retracting the landing gear after take-off.

Some other aircraft manufacturers also have PTUs, but the operations and sounds are different. You may also hear a high-pitched whine when the aircraft is at the gate before departure or after arrival. This is an electric hydraulic pump the ramp staff can use to open the cargo doors to get your bags unloaded.

WHAT ABOUT ANIMALS? HOW DO THEY TRAVEL?
Whilst you might not see animals in the passenger cabin very often, they can travel with you. However, for you to bring Rover the dog or Whiskers the cat on board, they must be a certified assistance or service animal. That means the animals that are trained as hearing/seeing eye dogs, stroke detectors, or animals for people suffering post-traumatic stress disorder (PTSD). For these animals to be carried there is official paperwork that must be submitted before the flight, and they have a seat blocked for them. No, it doesn't mean the animal will sit on the seat, it just ensures there is room for them and we can take into account the weight of the animal for planning purposes.

The animal must stay on a moisture-proof mat on the floor and be suitably restrained throughout the flight. There is also customs and quarantine issues depending on where you are flying to and from.

I have heard, but not seen, the practice of falcons, hawks and other birds of prey travelling in the passenger cabin. The sport of falconry is a popular pastime for the royal families and wealthy elite in the Middle East. They will often book a seat for their prized bird who will occupy a seat and sit on its perch with a cover over its head. The cover is designed to prevent the bird getting scared by being enclosed with other people around. Why haven't I seen it myself? Well because these pampered birds are usually in First Class, and I am not in any royal family!

Other bigger animals such as horses can be transported by air for horse racing, and zoos can often send animals to other zoos. These are primarily done on specific freight aircraft as they have the space available to carry them. On passenger aircraft, all the freight - including animals - goes in the hold underneath the passenger cabin, and it is usually not big enough for an adult to stand upright.

DO YOU EVER TRANSPORT DEAD BODIES? WHAT IF SOMEBODY DIES DURING THE FLIGHT?

This whilst certainly a macabre question, it is more surprising than you think. I am certain it will happen to us all eventually and you can never be sure where it will happen. Unfortunately, it can happen away from home, and deceased people have to be repatriated.

A body would be treated with utmost respect and dignity and would be inside a coffin placed into the aircraft hold. You can imagine it would be a distressful time if the family and friends of the deceased were also on board as passengers at the time. The airline would arrange for a discreet transfer to or from the cargo hold to an awaiting funeral home or hearse. This can also occur with ashes of somebody who has been cremated. The urn will also be carried in the hold.

Should somebody pass away in flight, the cabin crew would do their best to separate other passengers from the deceased. They would also cover the person with a curtain or blanket out of respect.

When an airline passenger plane travels, there is always a record of persons on board (POB). This may require amendment in flight to a number of POB and a number of souls. The reason for this is, in the unlikely event of an accident, emergency services need to know how many people they are looking for. This politely informs them that there is a deceased person on board.

CAN I FIND OUT ABOUT MY PILOT BEFORE I FLY? HOW LONG HAS HE OR SHE BEEN FLYING?

The best way is to ask the crew. You could ask them before the flight, if you see them walk through the terminal or ask the cabin crew as you board the aircraft. Certainly, don't be afraid to ask. We don't bite, and most crew are more than happy to tell you a bit about themselves. Sometimes it may be difficult to speak before a flight if the aircraft is on a short turnaround, which means after arrival it is quickly departing again. If you never ask, you will never know.

The savvy traveler knows:

- ✈ If you hate queuing, try to minimize the time you do so by checking in online. Usually the queue for bag drop is shorter and moves quicker.

- ✈ Listen to the P.A. Mostly they all sound the same but sometimes you will hear something that makes you laugh or hear something incorrect.

- ✈ Take a second to assess the security screening lanes. Shorter isn't always the quickest. Follow the business travelers or aircrew - they are the experts. Avoid the retirees and people with infants!

- ✈ Plan your own speedy journey through security. Look at the people ahead of you. Follow their lead as to what they are doing.

- ✈ Listen to the instructions of the staff doing the security checks. Think about your carry-on luggage: aerosols, gels, belts, shoes. If you are ready to go they may bring you to the front of the queue.

- ✈ It is ok to have a healthy fear of flying. You are reacting rationally. But consider your perception of the safety of airline travel is skewed. It really is the safest form of transport around. Your crew on board have a vested interest in getting you to your destination safely.

- ✈ Overbooking can happen. To avoid being offloaded, try to get to the airport early.

- ✈ Delays can happen. Put it in perspective that the crew are there to ensure the aircraft is 100% ready to go. You wouldn't want to take the chance of 99% ready!

- ✈ Relax. The barking dog is ok. Enjoy your flight. Marvel at the ability to take flight and defy the laws of gravity.

CHAPTER 2

DURING FLIGHT

CHECKLISTS

Checklists are a great tool to help us remember everything. It isn't like in the movies where one pilot calls out an item to another, and they both look up and complete and action. That is called a 'read and do' checklist.

Most of the things we do are completed as a scan, i.e. from memory. But the checklist is the double-check that it has been completed.

However, there are certain things pilots need to know and complete without any reference to checklists. These are called memory items or recall items. This is essential knowledge that needs to be completed in a real emergency. Hence, there is no time to reference a printed or electronic checklist. Relax, pilots practice these often. Personally, I have set of flash cards I review often to make sure they stay stuck in my mind.

We also have limitations that are committed to memory. This is dependent upon which aircraft you are flying but covers things like maximum take-off or maximum landing weights. It can be engine or oil temperature limits, or the maximum wind speeds doors can be opened in. It is all important information pilots need to know and commit to memory.

The checklist can be a little inbuilt system that can be pulled out and ticked off on the aircraft dashboard or glare shield. It can be a printed and laminated card that is read and responded to each time it is required.

On newer-generation aircraft like the Boeing 787 it can be fitted with an electronic checklist. It is accessed through the aircraft displays. It is a great tool that automatically knows which checklist is the next one in the queue. Should we have a non-normal situation that calls for a non-normal checklist, it guides the pilots through what to complete next and even remembers where you are up to in the list if you need to leave the checklist for any reason.

SEATBELTS
The bumps and when to keep your seatbelt on. In the planning stage, pilots will review weather and we have an idea of what the weather along our route will be like.

With this information we let the cabin crew know beforehand where bumps or turbulence is likely to occur. That being said, it is a little bit of a dark art rather than pure science. One of the things that can cause bumps is clear air turbulence or CAT. This is common at high altitudes where two or more air masses bump into each other and the resulting mixing causes the buffeting. There is a measure called shear rates, which compares the differences in wind speed and direction to give a numerical value. The higher this number rises, the likelihood of CAT increases. However, as mentioned earlier, you could be flying where the forecast shear rate is 1 or 2 with really rough weather then fly through and area of 6-7 and it can be smooth. All these figures are forecast so there is an element of estimating rather than hard facts.

So that is why you will hear pilots and cabin crew make announcements encouraging you to keep your seatbelt fastened even after the seatbelt sign has been extinguished. There have been accidents where aircraft have flown through turbulence or pitched abruptly and has sent unrestrained passengers hurtling around the cabin.

WHAT IS TURBULENCE? WILL IT CAUSE THE PLANE TO CRASH?
Turbulence is the thing that rattles the plane and your nerves, spills your beverage and assists in filling sick bags. Some people are quite terrified by the bumps that it often ranks as the number one fear for flyers.

In a way it does make some sense. You are in a pressurized aluminum tube, zooming through the sky at 6mi (12km) per minute and the air outside is -75F (-60C) and wouldn't have enough oxygen to support human life. Easy to picture that you are a vulnerable craft trapped in a hostile environment. Most people who step onto a plane have a little fear in the back of their minds. Yes, even pilots!

WHAT! You say I am not helping your fear of flying? Of course I have a fear of turbulence, I have a healthy respect for what I am doing and I, like all pilots, avoid what turbulence we can.

Each year a couple of hundred people are injured when an aircraft has encountered unexpected turbulence. Most of these injuries occur to cabin crew. We are aware they are the ones most likely to be walking around the most. They are part of the flight crew team and we will always try to look after them.

The bulk of these injuries are to head, neck, shoulders and ankles. So if you think about 100 or so injuries out of the several billion who fly each year, those are pretty good odds. If you keep your seatbelt fastened whenever you are seated, you will minimize the chance of this happening to you. And yes, that is why the air crew say that on most flights!

Unfortunately, that number will likely increase over time. There are now more people flying than ever before and everybody with a cell phone in their pocket has the ways and means to record the encounters. And those videos can be shared with the world before the aircraft has parked and shut down the engines. With the advent of inflight Wi-Fi, they will probably be shared before the pilots have communicated the incident to the company, Air Traffic Control, and other pilots.

Turbulence comes in varying levels and whilst it is frustrating and uncomfortable, it would be rare in the extreme for a plane to depart controlled flight by turbulence alone.

A plane cannot be flipped upside-down, thrown into a tail slide or spin by even the strongest gust or pocket of disturbed air. Even if this occurred, an airliner has a design characteristic called 'positive stability.' When an aircraft is disturbed from its position in space, its inherent nature is to go back to where it came from. In this case we would hope it would return to straight and level flight.

If the disturbances were extreme, the pilots would manually fly the aircraft to get it back to straight and level flight quickly. Jet upset training is covered in simulator training sessions and many pilots have done similar in a light aircraft. This involves putting the aircraft in some really uncommon attitudes, i.e. very high or low aircraft nose attitudes and large angles of bank, which is the rolling of the plane.

In these maneuvers, pilots are deliberately disorientated. They then have to recover to ensure they can do it in the unlikely event it occurred for real.

From my point of view, turbulence is uncomfortable and inconvenient. It is rare to be a safety issue. Just a concern if you need to go to the toilet or you suffer from motion sickness. The aircraft won't break up in flight, we just want you to have a good flight and fly again as it keeps us employed!

Most passengers have experienced a bumpy ride on a plane, the routine – but sometimes frightening – drops and rises or waggling wings pales into comparison to what an aircraft is subjected to when undergoing tests.

Aircraft wings aren't solid chunks of metal They do require a bit of flex in them. They actually have a lot more flex than you think, and aircraft manufacturers put their machines through rigorous testing.

Firstly, the manufacturers want to see or demonstrate how the wings behave under normal and exceptional loads during their life. To achieve this, they perform 'static tests.' The plane's wings receive loads of up to 1.5 times higher than they would ever encounter during passenger revenue services. There are some great YouTube videos of these tests being completed.

In December 2013, Airbus built a special static airframe of its A350 XWB Airbus for ultimate load testing. When the ultimate load was reached, the plane's wingtip deflection was over five meters! That means the wing was bent up at almost 90 degrees.

There is a final test that involves getting the aircraft wings to snap – this helps engineers find out their breaking point, and safeguards it well beyond the expected load-levels the aircraft will ever encounter.

As you can see planes are over-engineered to take a great deal of stress. The amount of turbulence required to make an engine or wing fall off is beyond the normal realms of flight. If you flew through a thunderstorm it is possible, but pilots are risk averse and give thunderstorms a wide berth for this very reason.

I have struggled to find any real evidence where turbulence has led to a crash, even inadvertently. In turbulence the aircraft attitude and speed will fluctuate slightly. It is unlikely that altitude will diverge much more than +/- 100feet. This would also apply to the aircraft pitch and angle of bank. In the course of day-to-day operation, it is rare for an aircraft to exceed a bank of 25 degrees or a pitch attitude of beyond 20 degrees nose up. In turbulence however, people will swear the aircraft went to 90 degrees and fell out of the sky. It is not the case, it just feels extreme.

Aircraft have a 'turbulence penetration speed' which, to put it simply, gives the best buffer over going too fast or slow. We can also request to fly at a different altitude and seek smooth air above or below us. Air Traffic Control can't always grant requests to change altitude due to conflicting traffic.

Case Study:
Our bumps were the best available.

Flying between Japan and Singapore one day I encountered some moderate turbulence. I was definitely being pushed and pulled against my seatbelt and it was starting to become difficult to touch the controls in one fluid motion.

We heard other pilots in our area reporting severe turbulence. We knew we couldn't do much as they were at different levels to us. We just had to ride it out.

Not very enjoyable but all the cabin crew and passengers were pre-briefed and strapped in as it was forecast to be bumpy in this area.

Avoiding turbulence is a little bit of a dark art. We study weather charts, forecasts, radar pictures, and reports from Air Traffic Control. We couple that with all the experience we have learned over the thousands of hours and nautical miles we have flown

As the aircraft rides through the bumps, you might think the pilots are furiously fighting the aircraft. Both gripping the control column or side stick and working up a sweat trying to wrest control back. In fact, sometimes the worst thing pilots can do is try to fight it. The autopilots can actually assist in providing a smoother ride by dampening down the control inputs.

This is not supported by media reporting of issues that do occur. The media can't get enough of aircraft that plummet or dive. In October 2017 an Air Asia plane departing Perth, Australia, suffered a loss of cabin pressure. The media reports splash: *fell out of the sky, plummeted, diving, terrain impact only moments away!*

This is categorically incorrect. The aircraft must return to an altitude quickly so people can breathe. There isn't enough oxygen at high altitude. The pilots get the aircraft down quickly by flying the aircraft within its design limits. A loss of cabin pressurization is also called an emergency descent, but it is still under control of the pilots. You will, however, descend from whatever altitude you were at to 10,000 feet in a few minutes versus a normal descent that could take 20 minutes.

There is also different types of turbulence the aircraft can be affected by. There is general turbulence, which is really just the mixing and creation of bumpy air. There is also clear air turbulence, which is even harder to forecast but often occurs in and around jet streams. A jet stream is just a long column of fast moving air. The air in these jet streams can be over 200mph or 350kph.

There is mechanical turbulence. This is a down-wind effect of obstacles in the path of the breeze. In my hometown of Melbourne, Australia, one of the runways is aligned to the south. Just to the west or right-hand side there is a small forest. When the wind blows from the south-west as it predominately does in Melbourne, this wind is disturbed by the trees. So at 500 feet it could be steady winds and a smooth flight path, then in the final 150 feet it gets bumpy. Pilots are concentrating the hardest the closer we are to touchdown so we are more likely to be ready for these bumps and react accordingly.

Wake turbulence is another type we can encounter. However, it is a little easier to predicate and rules have been created to prevent its occurrence. Let's say you have a 300,000 kg A380 flying past. That means that 300,000kg of air has been displaced to keep the aircraft aloft. All that air begins swirling and tumbling.

The higher-pressure air underneath the wing moves toward the lower pressure air on the upper surface. This causes something known as wing-tip vortices which, when conditions are right, can appear to be like a horizontal tornado. You can actually hear them as planes depart or are coming in to land.

Without going into an aerodynamic lesson, this phenomenon is strongest when the aircraft are slow, and the wings are creating the most lift. They gradually run out of energy and disperse but they can effect a following aircraft for up to several minutes.

If you are a much lighter aircraft, you can imagine flying through what amounts to a washing machine. Air traffic controllers have very specific times and distance to keep aircraft of different weights well separated. The bigger the preceding aircraft and the smaller the following, the larger the separation.

As a rough rule of thumb, the bigger the aircraft, the bigger the wake it creates. One of the worst culprits for wake turbulence creation is the Boeing 757. I haven't flown near many of these mid-sized aircraft in my travels. Apparently, it has a particular aerodynamic trait that produces a wake that is not commensurate with its size. So much so, that ATC will increase the wake turbulence category of the aircraft and impose greater time and distance restrictions than they would for a similar sized aircraft.

You may be looking outside the window of your aircraft now and notice it has fins, winglets or sharklets at the wingtips. This is a way aerodynamic engineers have increased aerodynamic efficiency (with a subsequent reduction in fuel burn). The winglets tend to dampen the strength of the wing-tip vortices.

Flying through wake turbulence can also happen up at altitude in the cruise. If pilots can see an aircraft is going to pass overhead, they know the wake will fall. To avoid the bumps, they will factor in which way the wind is blowing then fly upwind to hopefully avoid the turbulent air.

Helicopters can also produce wake turbulence. When you think about it a helicopter has wings that move through the air just like an aircraft albeit in a different plane of motion. It is not unheard of for helicopters to flip over stationery light aircraft whilst hovering or taxiing past.

Thermals can also cause turbulence. Thermals are pockets of hot air that are rising faster than the surrounding air. This doesn't tend to affect larger aircraft to the same degree as it does for turbo-prop regional aircraft.

Despite all the procedures and rules, most pilots have experienced an encounter with turbulence. It can run the whole gamut of the tail end of decaying vortices or a full-on shake, rattle and roll. It may only last momentarily, but they are unforgettable.

Case Study:

Don't get concerned when you hear the word turbulence.

Just think of it as bumpy air because that's all it really is.

WHY WOULD PILOTS WANT OR NEED TO DUMP OR JETTISON FUEL?

Airlines hate to waste fuel for no reason. It is often the biggest single expense for airlines in a year, notwithstanding the aircraft purchases themselves. Most larger jets can dump or jettison fuel

Great percentages of the time aircraft take off at a weight heavier than the maximum weight they can land at. They may actually carry more fuel than they weigh themselves.

As a comparison;

	Maximum Take-off weight	Max Landing Weight
Airbus A380	575,000kg	394,000kg
Boeing B787	228,000kg	172,365kg

So should there be a requirement (i.e. an emergency) to return to land not long after take-off, the pilots will go through a procedure to dump or jettison fuel. The requirement to return is usually serious like a heavy bird strike or an engine failure, not because you left your passport at the airport bar or duty-free shops!

As you can see from the table and a scenario above, an aircraft could be in a situation where it has to return to land heavier than it is designed to do. This would cause undue stress of the aircraft, in particular the undercarriage components (wheels, brakes and tires).

There are rules for jettisoning fuel. It is done at altitude (above 6000 feet) so it has a chance to disperse in the atmosphere and not rain down on the people below. It isn't done over built-up areas or in a holding pattern. Approval is generally sought from Air Traffic Control and the airline operations.

The jettison nozzles are at the back of the wing where the air that has been disturbed by the aircraft flying through it will greatly assist in dispersing the fuel through the atmosphere so it doesn't reach the ground. The nozzles are away from the exhaust areas of the engines as you would not want it to ignite and put the aircraft, passengers and crew into further danger. The rate at which the aircraft can dump fuel varies greatly, as do the mechanisms that activate it. And for those nervous flyers there, yes there are measures to automatically turn it off so all the fuel is not pumped overboard!

WHAT ARE THE TRAILS OF MIST AT THE WINGTIPS? ARE WE LOOSING FUEL?

There is no way an airline would deliberately pump fuel overboard unless necessary. As the previous section is about fuel jettison/dumping, I won't go over old ground. This isn't fuel but water vapor. There are also some grand conspiracy theories that refer to these as 'chemtrails' and the governments are spraying mind-control drugs over the population. You can judge its validity yourself, but refer to them as wing-tip vortices.

At the wing tips, there is a mixing of high and low-pressure air. The high-pressure underneath seeks out the area of lower pressure above the wing. This makes a tight little spinning mass of air almost like a sideways cyclone or tornado. I also touch on this area in turbulence and wake turbulence.

When all the atmospherics are in the right mix of temperature, pressure and humidity, the moisture in these mini tornados condenses and becomes visible. Up close they do look like mini tornados. When the aircraft is up at altitude, they look like smoke trails (or chemtrails depending on who you believe).

If you are in flight it is highly unlikely you will see these trails from your own aircraft. However, this condensation can occur around other parts of the aircraft. Quite often when coming in to land you will see the phenomenon occur around flaps and slats and the engine pylons.

WHAT DO ALL THE LETTERS AND NUMBERS MEAN ON THE GROUND WHEN WE ARE TAXIING?

For most passengers, seeing blue lights or yellow lines outside a plane's window is your reminder to turn your phone back on. All the colors and letters you can see outside actually mean different things.

These are like street names but limited to a few letters. They allow pilots to taxi and Air Traffic Control to tell us which route they want us to travel.

Yes, Air Traffic Control is not just confined to the air, we are also controlled on the ground. This controller can be called ground or surface movement control. The first time they are contacted the airport name will be used, for example 'Sydney Ground' or 'Singapore Ground.' For any subsequent contact, 'Ground' will usually suffice.

The controllers do a complicated ballet moving aircraft around. They ensure an aircraft that pushes back doesn't impede an aircraft taxiing to a parking bay. They navigate the aircraft from its gate to the take-off runway and, conversely, they assist aircraft that have completed a landing to taxi to their parking gates.

If you have ever looked out across taxiways at an airport, you will see most aircraft taxiing the same way or direction. Airports tend to have standard routes. This can help to reduce workload for controllers and pilots as we have an expectation of what to expect. It also means the length of radio transmissions are reduced freeing up the radio waves.

If you have a look outside (I am assuming you are reading this on a flight, if not, next time you are flying somewhere) you will see little signs in yellow and black. It can be black letters on a yellow background or yellow letters on a black background like this:

A way to remember this is 'all black, on that track.' So in the example above the aircraft is taxiing along taxiway Alpha and if we turn right at the next taxiway, we will turn onto Bravo. I explain about A=Alpha and B=Bravo in a few pages.

Large black numbers on a yellow background indicate how much runway distance remains. Pilots may do an intersection departure, which means taking off without using the entire runway to save time. This distance marker confirms to the pilot that they are in the correct intersection.

If you see white numbers on red backgrounds, they are meant to act as stop signs. It is annotating that it is possibly an active runway.

You may also see the runway number followed by a letter. Runway nomenclature is determined by the magnetic bearing of the runway center line. Runway numbers will only ever go as high as 36 as there are only 360 degrees. If the bearing is 080, the runway can be runway 8 or 08 depending upon the country you are in. Where does the letter fit in? If there are two or more parallel runways a letter is added to differentiate them from one another.

These are also depicted in charts or maps that we carry on board. They were once physical manuals that had hundreds of pages but now they have moved to the digital age. They can be viewed on iPads or even in integrated electronic flight bags built into the aircraft itself.

The latest generation of aircraft (B787 and A350) have moving maps. This encompasses a database with all the airport information to permit the display of all these taxiways to pilots on navigation displays. They greatly assist in helping pilots to taxi aircraft, particularly in conditions of low visibility.

You may also see a lot of different markings. This isn't a manual to teach you to recognize all of them. Just a couple that you are bound to see on every flight you take.

DO YOU REALLY FLY IT OR IS IT THE AUTOPILOT?

A mixture of both. There is certainly a high level of automation and pilots have become systems managers and technical experts rather than flying aces with superior stick and rudder skills. The autopilot certainly does a more efficient job flying in the cruise. It is not unlike cruise control in a car on a freeway. But pilots are still controlling and monitoring the aircraft, just like a driver still controls a car whilst cruise control is active.

We are not the back-up system in case the automatics fail. The aircraft doesn't control itself. It is responding to the inputs the pilots command.

Modern airliners are known as fly-by-wire. Earlier generations of aircraft relied on wires and pulleys connected to the moving parts of the plane and the pilot's control columns. This meant the pilots were responsible for keeping the aircraft within the realms of safe flight.

In newer aircraft, pilots still move controls – be it a side stick or conventional column. However, these movements make requests to flight computers to move the flight control surfaces. The direct mechanical link between the flight control surface and the pilots' controls has pretty much been removed.

There are many ill-informed articles published saying that pilots only 'fly' the aircraft for a few minutes on every flight. The fact they are published often doesn't make it true. This adds weight to the assertions that pilotless aircraft are a short-term inevitability.

These are merely headline-grabbers that lead to misunderstanding by the travelling public of what an airliner can actually achieve. Yes, it is true that we only hand fly for short periods of time. The autopilots do that function much more efficiently. We are no longer controlling the aircraft with control column or side stick inputs, which is the 'hand flying' part. However, just about everything the plane achieves is done so under instruction from the pilots. The plane still goes where we tell it to, in the way we want it to. If we need to climb or descend, there are various methods to achieve this depending upon the requirements of weather, other traffic, Air Traffic Control and time. We will use one of the modes that is appropriate, and the autopilot flies it the way we want it to. In that way pilots aren't hand flying, but we are flying through the autopilot and are more like system managers.

The aircraft cannot think for itself. In fact, having two pilots leads to better outcomes as far as safety and efficiency is concerned. One pilot can challenge the thinking or actions of the other to ensure the best course of action. A computer can't think for itself...well, not yet anyway.

There are thoughts that I discuss in another part of the book about whether automation will see pilots engineered out of the flight deck.

It is often cited that in a similar way that technology greatly assists medical professionals, the technology and automation greatly assists pilots to fly better. The difference is how the pilots use the technology.

In the same way you would not want a surgical robot doing an operation on you without intervention by a human, you wouldn't want a robot flying you to your destination without a human in the cockpit. When I am asked about this by passengers or friends, I always put it to them: wouldn't you prefer to have people up there who are just as heavily invested in a safe outcome as you?

There is also some confusion about what the autopilot can actually do. Autopilots can certainly conduct automatic landings (abbreviated to auto-lands in pilot lingo). It requires a certain amount of training in equipment of the aircraft and airport. It is not a given that each landing will be an auto-land, in fact they are quite rare as it is not as simple as just pushing a button. There are a lot more rules and requirements. But the capability is certainly an asset in low-visibility conditions like fog. All take-offs are manual. There is no such a thing as an auto take-off.

I would certainly agree there are times the automation will do a much better job than I can. It can process information quicker and isn't prone to fatigue and distractions. However, pilot error can often be cited as reason for crashes. What is not often heard is where pilots have been able to make decisions that have prevented a crash or near miss. That won't make the headlines.

Even the cabin crew who work closely alongside us are not fully aware of how busy the flight deck can become. The cabin crew only come up to the flight deck when the seat belt sign is off. Certainly, in the cruise it is a period of low workload and we may appear to be not doing much. The automatics are doing what they are supposed to do.

Our busiest period in the flight deck is on departure and on descent to land, and we only have required crew on the flight deck to minimize distractions.

Particularly on descent and approach there are a number of competing and conflicting demands. ATC may need us to slow down but due to wind changes we may also need to increase descent. These are two mutually exclusive actions. If we try to achieve one outcome it will make the other worse. We may need to avoid bad weather and reduce or increase descent at the same time. Pilots will often say we need to be ahead of the aircraft and we would try to anticipate this scenario and what our actions would be, not merely react to it when it presents. The autopilot will be doing what we tell it to do as we process all the other information and requirements coming in.

To that end, computers cannot think for themselves...yet. They are a great assistance to the pilots, not the other way around.

WHAT DO YOU DO IF THERE IS BAD WEATHER ON OUR FLIGHT PATH?

This occurs so regularly that it is more noteworthy when flights don't have any bad weather. This would come back to the pilots' pre-flight planning stage. We have a pretty good idea of weather that is en route from forecasts and satellite pictures. Obviously, the satellite pictures are old news by the time we reach certain areas, but pilots are always thinking ahead.

If there was an area of bad weather, we would hopefully know about it before we even take-off. During the flight we would build our situational awareness well in advance, scanning the weather radar for areas of thunderstorms or possible turbulence.

Once an area was identified, we would seek clearance from ATC to deviate from our cleared flight plan. This happens well in advance of reaching the area. A good rule of thumb we use is have it actioned by 80nm (160km). Seems like a fair distance away. If you are travelling at 6nm (12km) a minute that space will be travelled in about 10 minutes. We may need to inform the cabin crew to pack away a meal service and that can take about 10 minutes.

Case Study:
Good weather en route is rare.

In the last 5 years I have done about 2-3 medium-haul flights per week. That is flights between 5-12 hours in duration.

Multiply those numbers and take away a few for vacations and illness. That will give you a rough idea of how many flights I have done.

Out of all those flights, I think there have been three or four where I have experienced no bad weather on our route. That means a handful of times I have not had to seek permission from ATC to fly off track to avoid that weather.

Lesson: Pilots avoid bad weather.

WHAT IF WE GET HIT BY LIGHTNING?

Again, I will emphasize pilots are conservative by nature and experience. We will give thunderstorms a wide berth. *A wide berth*. I added that twice for emphasis.

But lightning is unpredictable and can shoot out the side of thunderstorms, and aircraft do get hit probably more often than you realize. There are plenty of images and videos on the internet of aircraft being hit by lightning. The aircraft still flies.

Case Study:
Did we really get hit?

I remember flying one night and we flew close to some thunderstorms but we were still 20-30 miles away from the most active part of the storm.

There were plenty of bright flashes, but the flight path was smooth as we were upwind of the thunderstorm.

After an uneventful flight the engineers met the aircraft on arrival and told us we had been hit by lightning. They could see the missing static wicks, and then proceeded to look for the tell-tale sign of the strike.

I went down for a look as I didn't know we'd been hit. The point on the aircraft where the bolt obviously hit left a little singe mark and a tiny hole a couple of millimeters across. If I hadn't had it pointed out to me, I wouldn't have seen it.

This was one example where we were not even aware we had been hit. Other times you may but the point is the aircraft will keep flying.

A lightning bolt is obviously a big charge of electricity and if it hits an aircraft that charge needs to go somewhere and will follow the path of least resistance.

All airliners have little things on the trailing edges called static discharge wicks. If you look out your window, you will see lots of little things that look like straws on the back of the wing.

If the bolt hits the aircraft the charge will flow down and out through these little wicks. They are sacrificial in so far as if the bolt does travel through them, they will most certainly be blown off. But that is ok, there are plenty of them. Aircraft have between 30-50 of them.

CAN PILOTS FLY MORE THAN ONE TYPE OF AIRLINER?

This is another yes/no answer. A pilot who flies a Boeing 737 can fly different variants of the 737. It could be a 737-400 series one day and a 737-800 series the next.

Case Study:

How do I know what aircraft I am on now?

Pull out the safety briefing card from the seatback pocket and it will tell you!

Not having flown either of these Boeing aircraft, I can assume they are very similar but not the same. I have flown an Airbus A320 and an A321, switching between both. From the cockpit, they are basically the same aircraft. For the record, the A321 is heavier and has more seats.

A pilot may have previously been endorsed on an Airbus A320 and a Boeing 737. They are qualified to fly both but generally will not fly both types. Different variants of a type, i.e. a series you can but not different aircraft. I have also flown an Airbus A330 and it, too, is remarkably similar to the other Airbus aircraft my airline has operated (A320 and A321) but I didn't switch between both types.

From a risk assessment point of view, it is too risky having a pilot fly both. Without going into the minutiae of operating an airliner, there are certain things that each aircraft manufacturer does differently. An action on one aircraft may require a switch or knob to be pulled, whereas another it may be pushed to complete the same action.

We also have a thing called 'mouth music.' It is a take on Standard Operating Procedures (SOPs), and what is said and when. Again, each aircraft and airline differs with regard to what is said and when it is said. By keeping pilots flying on the same aircraft, it minimizes the risk of human error and a pilot saying the wrong thing.

But for all the nervous flyers, reading this book, it also means your pilot up front is an expert on their machine!

HOW DO YOU TALK IN ISOLATED AREAS? WHAT HAPPENS IF YOU LOSE RADIO CONTACT?

Fortunately, we have multiple back-up ways to communicate. Most voice communication is done over VHF radio, which works on line-of-sight or a little bit longer (about 7%). There is a specific formula that can be used to calculate the theoretical range. An aircraft up at altitude has a pretty good range. As an example, an aircraft operating between 30,000 and 40,000 feet will have VHF ranges of between 213-246nm or 400km.

For those of you who haven't been to Australia, it is a big country with lots of vast, uninhabited space. It would be cost prohibitive to put transmitters everywhere to guarantee radio coverage at all times. Those transmitters would require maintenance, the cost of which would be passed onto the airline, which in turn would be added to the price of your ticket. About 80% of the population live within one hour of the coast. This means there are large areas where there isn't VHF radio coverage.

Then there are the rather large bodies of water that make up 70% of the world's surface. There isn't much VHF coverage between Australia and the United States.

Older aircraft would make position reports so the air traffic controllers would have a fair idea of what time they will pop back into radio coverage. In the interim, an HF frequency could be used. You wouldn't listen to HF frequency for all this time. There is a lot of background interference and noise.

Pilots turn it on when they need to transmit, then off again once it is complete. There is also a way for ATC to contact us by ringing a specific code that each aircraft has. If you get this thing called a SELCAL, the radio is then listened to again until the message is received and understood.

More modern aircraft use a system called CPDLC - Controller Pilot Data Link Communications. Best way to describe it is sending text messages back and forth between controller and pilots. Most messages are generic, as we are asking for something specific – clearance to deviate around weather or to climb/descend to another altitude. There is an ability to type free text in also, but it is used sparingly to avoid misunderstanding.

So, should an aircraft lose radio contact, a pilot would try all the other VHF radios, then maybe a HF radio or CPDLC (see previous question). Failing that, pilots would enter a special code into a transponder that lets Air Traffic Control, and more recently the general public, see us. Have a look at https://www.flightview.com/flighttracker/

What is the code and how do we remember it? 7600. Seventy-six...radio fix is how I was taught to remember it! We can also use other codes to indicate other emergencies should they be required.

WHAT CALL SIGN DO THEY GIVE YOU?

For commercial airline flights, the aircraft will use the airline name followed by the flight number. Yes, the same one that is on your ticket/boarding pass. So Jetstar One from Melbourne to Honolulu gets called 'Jetstar One' on radio transmissions. Most airlines have the call sign of the company name but there are some exceptions. Tigerair previously used 'Gocat,' British Airways uses 'Speedbird,' and China Airlines uses 'Dynasty.'

English is the International Aviation Language standard. Again, there are exceptions. Chinese carriers speak Chinese to their carriers. Flying into China, I always found it a bit unnerving as you aren't sure what is going on with other aircraft. I seriously commend the air traffic controllers there, though, with the ease with which they flick between Chinese and English. In France, I think they also speak French to Air France, but I am not certain as I haven't flown there myself...yet.

WHAT DOES ALL THE ALPHA BRAVO CHARLIE ZULU MEAN?

This is called the phonetic alphabet. It allows spelling to be completed over a radio transmission that may not be clear.

A number of letters can be pronounced or sound similar to others. This is especially the case if English is not the primary language. Imagine C and Z, E or T, E or P.

So each letter of the alphabet has its own word so no two letters sound the same. What are they?

The Phonetic Alphabet

A – Alpha	J – Juliet	S – Sierra
B – Bravo	K – Kilo	T – Tango
C – Charlie	L – Lima	U – Uniform
D – Delta	M – Mike	V – Victor
E – Echo	N – November	W – Whiskey
F – Foxtrot	O – Oscar	X – X-ray
G – Golf	P – Papa	Y – Yankee
H – Hotel	Q – Quebec	Z – Zulu
I – India	R – Romeo	

When I was younger this was the thing I was most concerned about remembering when I was investigating learning to fly!

Whilst researching for this book, I discovered the medical profession use the phonetic alphabet for patient identification numbers also!

WHAT HAPPENS IF YOU HIT A BIRD?

Bird strikes are unfortunately an outcome of occupying the same airspace at the same time. Usually it is more unfortunate for the bird. It can also happen to bats around dusk and dawn.

Bird strikes normally occur in terminal areas at lower altitudes. That is, areas around airports as aircraft are departing or arriving. Birds don't often fly up at aircraft cruise altitudes, but strikes have been recorded as high as 6mi/11km. However, it is down at lower levels where they generally happen. Birds could be scanning the ground looking for prey etc., and are not expecting a much larger, faster 'bird' to bear down on them.

Alternatively, flocks of birds could fly across the path of an aircraft, oblivious to the flight path.

If you were a bird, a large open green space - seemingly devoid of humans and other predators – would be a nice place to reside. Airport operators do their best to manage the threat of bird strike and the welfare of flying animals. The best option is to keep aircraft and birds apart from each other.

Culling has been used before, but animal rights activists oppose these measures. The more humane ways to move the birds on is to use measures to frighten them away. Birds of prey can be trained to scare aware other birds. Airports may also employ scarecrows or random noise generators, distress calls, and firing of flares to discourage birds from staying in the area.

If a period of mass migration or nesting is occurring, aerodrome operators will put out a NOTAM (Notice to Airman) informing pilots of the situation. That said, there is not much pilots can do about it apart from being aware. The best thing we can do is to ensure our aircraft is visible to any airborne creatures. This entails flying at a speed that allows birds the opportunity to move out of the way, and also to have lights on. When flying below 10,000 feet, most airlines have a standard operating procedure to have lights on and fly below 250knots, to facilitate this.

So, what happens if a bird is struck? The bird, depending on the size, will just disintegrate. The worst time to hit one is on take-off. The aircraft is quite robust and is designed and constructed to withstand bird strikes. You can certainly search online video recordings of windshield resistance testing. In these tests, bird type objects (weights and dimensions – not real birds) are fired out of a canon at the aircraft.

The aircraft won't suffer too much unless the bird flies into one of the engine intakes. This could cause an engine failure.

Pilots do recurrent training in full-motion simulators to practice dealing with events like bird strikes. Engine failures on take-off are practiced most of the time. We can even practice bird strikes with the visuals (outside the cockpit) showing a flock of birds flying towards the aircraft.

Is it realistic? Absolutely! Recently I was conducting type rating training to qualify a pilot onto the Boeing 787, and I programed a bird strike. As the bird flew in front of us in the simulator, he actually ducked his head. As he was previously a fighter pilot – a bird strike could smash into the canopy and it was a natural reaction for him. We had a bit of a chuckle about it afterwards. (Sorry Chris, too funny not to mention!)

In my own flying career, I have probably had about a dozen bird/bat strikes. Most of the events I have actually been unaware of hitting anything due to the location of the strike and size of the bird that has been hit. It has been the engineers who, after inspecting the aircraft on arrival, have informed the crew that we hit something.

If a bird strike occurs on approach to land, it is not as concerning as the aircraft has speed and momentum to continue to fly.

I gather you know about the 2009 story US Airways Flight 1549, also known as the 'Miracle on the Hudson,' which has also been made into a movie - *Sully*. Tom Hanks played the part of Captain Chesley 'Sully' Sullenberger, who safely guided his aircraft to a water 'landing' (officially called a 'ditching') after flying through a flock of geese and suffering a double engine failure.

Fortunately, engine failures after bird strikes are rare. Double engine failures after bird strike are almost unheard of.

ARE AIRCRAFT GERM LABS?

The belief of aircraft being known as germ factories has become more pronounced recently. With the quick spread of communicable diseases such as Ebola and SARS gaining widespread media attention, it is often cited as a passenger(s) flew in/arrived at a place recently via a flight from....

It probably serves to highlight why people are concerned about things you can catch on a flight. However, those same travelers probably don't think twice about catching public transport on a day-to-day basis.

Cabin air is filtered and should remove most airborne bacteria and viruses. In a modern airliner, the air is a mix of fresh and recirculated. In reality, it only takes about three minutes to refresh the aircraft. When an aircraft undergoes certification, it must be able to clear (pump out) smoke in a certain time frame. This is a lot faster than you would have in another public space.

So your chances of catching something from a sick person are pretty slim unless they cough, sneeze etc., directly on/over you.

Now the air is clean but what about the aircraft bathrooms? The cabin crew will try to keep them clean and well stocked. Depending upon the carrier and where you are sitting, you could be sharing your facility with 50 others. If it's a long flight, that adds up to a great many visits to a cramped little space. Assuming everybody has fantastic hygiene habits, it only takes a little turbulence, to...ahh...throw off a guy's aim or splash water from the sink etc. Or hands may not be washed at all. So just touching the door handle can expose you to who knows what. And I am amazed at the number of people who visit the bathroom without shoes!

The best way to beat these nasties is to have some hand sanitizer gel or wipes. The wipes are also great to wipe down your tray table and seat belt.

After saying all that, you should never fly with a head cold. Aircrews are well aware of the dangers of flying with a cold or congestion/blocked sinuses.

As the aircraft climbs, the cabin altitude rises and the ambient air pressure reduces. If you have blockages in your upper respiratory tract, the air inside your inner ear will slowly leak out. You will probably hear and feel it. It squeaks and leaks to equalize the pressure. That part is ok. However, when the aircraft reaches its top of descent, you can be in real trouble.

The situation you will have now is the ambient air pressure is increasing and it will be trying to get into your inner ear to equalize this. But as you have blockages, it can't happen. Therefore, the thin membrane of your ear drums will be put under a great deal of stress. It is agony when you can't equalize. (It also explains why young children and babies can start crying/screaming then all of a sudden stop.) Cabin crew may hand out sweets for kids to chew or suck. By wiggling your jaw (or chewing/swallowing) it can help to break the seal and allow the air pressure to equalize.

Please, if you take away one piece of advice from this book, please don't fly with a cold. The above is painful, if the aircraft was to depressurize, you would in all likelihood perforate your ear drums. I am not a doctor, I think they can get repaired, but you will be in agony.

CAN YOU GET SUCKED IN OR STUCK ON THE TOILET SEAT?

Theoretically, this is possible. However, it would require you to sit down and ensure you had a perfect unbroken seal between your backside and the seat. You would then have to contort your body around to flush. The toilets work on a vacuum or suction system. So the fear is that it could start and the negative pressure could, uhm, suck you onto the seat.

The chances of this happening are pretty remote. Firstly, you would have to be a certain size that could completely form a seal around the seat. The seat itself has air pockets underneath that would prevent a seal forming. So you would have to lift the seat up and sit on an exposed toilet, which is kind of gross. Then if the suction did occur, the human body is made up of movable muscle and tissue fibers, so they would probably move with the suction, thereby breaking the seal and preventing you getting stuck. (The lawyers told me to insert some sort of caveat here that warns you if you do try this I cannot be held responsible.)

WHEN YOU THE FLUSH THE TOILET, DOES IT GO INTO THE AIR?

No. The aircraft has a tank up the back of the aircraft that stores all the waste from the sinks and bathrooms.

There are some aircraft where the sinks discharge overboard. As the sinks are generally not in use until the aircraft is at altitude, this small amount of water is dispersed into the atmosphere. If the sink is used on the ground, water will run out onto the tarmac. Doing a pre-flight walk around, I avoid walking under these drains for obvious reasons.

There are warnings not to flush anything other than tissue paper down them. I have heard of a case where an infants' nappy was sucked into the waste system. It went down but then got stuck halfway.

This causes that toilet to become unserviceable for the remainder of that flight. Then the engineers will have to work out how to get the offending item out. This can involve a long process, as they first have to find where it got stuck.

IS IT POSSIBLE FOR SOMEBODY TO OPEN A CABIN DOOR MID-FLIGHT?

There are often media reports of passengers who have gone a bit crazy and tried to open doors during flight. There will be some hyperbole added to the reports. Eyewitness accounts will be added, and who will no doubt mention how close it all came to being catastrophic.

However, the reports will often fail to mention that it is impossible to do so. This is even the case when the aircraft is pressurized on the ground. The aircraft pressurization – or what is more commonly known as the laws of physics – won't allow it.

Airline transport aircraft fly where the air (oxygen) is too thin for humans to breathe unaided. So the aircraft is pumped up like a football to retain an atmosphere similar to what humans experience back on terra firma, albeit at a slightly higher altitude – around the 6-8000 feet mark.

Now imagine this football requires doors. If the doors opened outwards, it would be extremely difficult to keep them closed. I am sure it could be done, but the engineering that would be required to ensure the doors remain closed would add a significant weight penalty to the aircraft. More weight means more fuel burn, which means more expensive tickets.

Now imagine the doors opened inwards, into the football, just like aircraft doors. Now these doors act like plugs. The force of the pressurization keeps them in place. It would be impossible for a human to overcome the force of the pressurization system.

At cruising altitudes, there can be up to 8 pounds of pressure pushing against the entire surface inside the aircraft. That works out to over 1000 pounds against each square meter of the doors. More than any human could overcome. And there are also physical, mechanical, electric and hydraulic mechanisms that hold the door in place. So even down at lower altitudes it would still be too much force for a person to override.

You can just trust me on this. Or alternatively, ask the cabin crew if they have ever had anybody try to open a door, and whether they were successful or not. But first tell them you were reading a book, least they think you are about to try. If you do try it, you may get wrestled to the ground by concerned passengers. In this case just take my word for it.

SO HOW DO THE DOORS GET OPENED IN AN EMERGENCY?

The situation on the ground is a little different in the event of an emergency. If an evacuation is likely, the pilots will be going through a very methodical checklist that gets the plane ready for everybody to get out quickly. Yes, you certainly don't want to jump in front of a jet engine that is still running!

One of the items on that list is to manually depressurize the plane. This deflates the aircraft (football, in our analogy) to ambient pressure. So, it is the same on the outside and inside. Then there is no residual resistance. The doors can now be opened in order to start an evacuation.

You may hear the announcements to: 'arm doors and cross check' or to 'disarm doors and cross check.' Again, each airline is different, but the outcome is still the same. What the cabin crew is doing in these two scenarios is preparing for passengers to disembark.

The first scenario will be for an emergency evacuation. The doors and emergency slides are ready to be activated by the cabin crew in the event of an emergency evacuation. The second is a normal procedure, whereby the cabin crew are disarming the automatics so when the doors are opened to allow the passengers to be disembarked, the emergency slides don't deploy.

Yes, it has certainly happened before that slides have been inadvertently activated. It is embarrassing for the airline and certainly for the crew who make the mistake. The slides unfurl really quickly and with enough force to cause injuries or fatalities, and could also severely damage aerobridges. However, humans can make errors and can suffer from fatigue. These events probably occur a few times a year.

RECLINING SEATS

I would guess that this query really pertains to the cabin and the person sitting in front of you. Pilots can recline their seats, but it isn't done during take-off and landing just like the passengers.

It is certainly the norm the economy class seats recline, and most people feel it is slightly more comfortable than to be sitting ram-rod straight for a lengthy period. The issue of seat-recline is becoming more and more of an issue, though, and the cause of air-rage.

During take-off and landing, the seats must be upright. This allows everybody to get out of their seats quickly and evacuate safely should the need arise. However, once the seatbelt sign has been extinguished, passengers are free to recline their seats to the fully aft position.

On a short flight or during meal service it is generally considered poor form to recline your seat. With airlines constantly trying to eke out better yields and filling planes with cheaper airfares, the room between seat rows is reducing. I have seen many occasions of passengers with wet or sticky pants after the person in front launches a seat right back with no warning – the previously-balanced drinks now adorning the clothing of the unlucky soul behind.

Should you ask permission to recline? No, I don't think so but if meals are being served, it is certainly polite to raise the seat. Personally, if I recline my seat, I will try to do it slowly and in stages to allow the person behind me time to relocate drinks and/or laptops etc.

The other easier work-around to avoid seat rage...fly business class! This might be harder on your wallet though!

This phenomenon has also seen rise to a device being sold called a knee defender. It basically prevents the person in front from reclining their seat. I am certain this will cause further air rage incidents and will lead to airlines banning their use.

Seat-recline rage can also go the opposite way. This occurs when the person behind grabs the seat back each time they hop in and out of their seats. Grabbing the seat back can become annoying, particularly if the person in front is, or is trying, to sleep.

With reduced spaces between rows, sometimes it cannot be helped. There just isn't enough room to maneuver. If you must, try to be gentle or use the arm rests for leverage.

It can also materialize with seat back entertainment and the screen being pushed hard and the force going through the seat back. Avoid this by using the hand controller if one is provided.

AIR RAGE AND AIR FRUSTRATION
What is it that makes seemingly normal people behave in less than ideal ways? Going on vacation should be a relaxing time, but the whole process of arriving at the airport can sometimes feel as though control is being taken away from you. You are at the mercy of somebody else, and it can make people frustrated.

In no particular order of experience or magnitude of frustration, there is: getting to the airport, and associated costs of transport or parking; the lining up - for check in, security screening, passport control/immigration, and boarding the plane itself. Over-priced food, drink, and gee don't get me started on what it costs to hire a luggage trolley in Australia!

There is nothing you can do about these.

This phenomenon is not confined to the economy-class cabin either. In late 2014 a Korean Airline executive, Heather Cho, went berserk at the cabin crew after being unhappy with the way she was served nuts. They were served in the original packaging and she wanted them on a plate. She ordered the aircraft to taxi back to the gate before take-off. After an ongoing heated discussion with the Chief Cabin Crew member, she assaulted him, which necessitated a return to the gate and an eventual delay to the aircraft departure.

After this incident became public, the executive and Korean Airlines were widely criticized. She was forced to resign from her position and was also sentenced to a year in prison for an offence against aviation safety.

What makes a seemingly intelligent person go crazy? There is often no escalation, just straight out attack. Alcohol can be a factor, and everybody knows travelling can be stressful, even if you are travelling for a vacation.

I see it as I walk through a terminal. Partners snap at each other and parents react to children's behavior with less tolerance than they would normally. I have been guilty of it myself.

So how do you stop it? I guess the best method is to prepare and be aware. Preparation means arriving early. That way any minor delays do remain that - minor and inconsequential. If you feel your hackles starting to rise, pause, take a couple of deep breaths, and then react.

Ok, so the flight has ended, now you may cross paths with the baggage carousel cozy-uppers. I am 100% certain that your bags will not come out any quicker the closer you are to the baggage carousel. Often the people who do push themselves or their trolleys right up close, invariably end up getting hit with other people's suitcases and nobody goes out of their way to assist them either! Maybe it's a karma thing?

Some airports have a line to try and get everybody to stand back. It doesn't always work. The bags will come. Take a deep breath and be patient, you have come this far.

Please try to put all this in perspective. You have flown in a low air pressure environment in a pumped-up aluminum tube at 80% of the speed of sound for a fraction of what it once cost. Perspective. If another passenger is angry or about to lose it, it is not about you. Is it worth escalating? Probably not. Step back. Focus on your vacation. Meditate. Don't get upset.

Case Study
Don't think you are big-noting yourself.

I remember a time flying from Melbourne to Darwin. For those not in Australia, it is about a four-hour flight up through the middle of Australia.

Whilst completing our pre-flight procedures, the Cabin Manager, Claire, came in to inform us we had a passenger who was possibly going to give us some trouble.

The specifics of what he did, I can't remember, but cabin crew have a gut feel. The passenger was obviously not happy about something and everybody else was bearing the brunt of his bad mood.

He opted to put himself in the emergency exit row, a seat he hadn't been allocated. There were discussions about this with the cabin crew. He was politely asked to move to his allocated seat. He did so eventually. But again, expressed his displeasure to everybody else within earshot, and his language sounded colorful to say the least.

Whilst walking to his seat he barged past other people and was just rude and obnoxious. He was not the least bit concerned about hitting other people with his bags or berating others for being in his way. He then demanded the cabin crew lift his bags into the overhead locker (that isn't their job by the way). He then complained loudly, using coarse language about airline service etc.

He was going to be a pain. Claire came in and informed the Captain and myself of his behavior, and said she wasn't happy having this guy on board for a four-hour flight. We informed the ground staff he had to be removed, and they started the off-loading process.

Let's just say he wanted to shoot the messenger when the news was delivered to him. He was given the ultimatum that he could walk off willingly, or the Federal Police were on the way to assist. He continued with his language and abuse of all staff, informing of his intent to sue.

As he walked off the plane, all the other passengers clapped. Apparently, he had been a pain in the boarding gate also. His poor wife/partner walked off the plane quite sheepishly, no doubt extremely embarrassed by his behavior.

In a further show of support to Claire and the other cabin crew, passengers willingly gave written statements. They also shared their contact details in case he did try to sue. What he would sue for I am not sure, but I am not a lawyer!

So you might not be happy but don't think the passengers are going to side with you. They want to get to their destination in peace and quiet.

After the event, I gave Claire the nickname 'Kick'em off Claire', and we found out that because the guy had caused a delay, he forfeited his fare. Expensive trip when you don't even depart!

I SAW MY PILOT IN THE GALLEY – WHO IS FLYING?

Now, pilots basically stay in the cockpit unless we are visiting the bathroom or going on a break. Two pilots are required but we go visit the bathroom in periods of low workload. At this time the autopilot is flying, and the other pilot is managing the radios and the flying. Normally one pilot flies the aircraft and the other looks after the radios. In a period of low workload, i.e. cruise, it is feasible that one pilot can complete both roles.

Some airlines/aircraft are almost self-contained, with their own crew rest facilities and toilets. I have never seen one, so I am not sure how common that set up is or whether it is a bit of an urban legend. Most airlines want as much space on the plane for revenue, so a separate toilet facility for crew is probably seen as an excessive waste of space these days.

Additionally, since 9/11, there has been an increase in pilots developing kidney stones. This terror attack lead to the installation of heavy bulletproof doors being installed on commercial airliners. This is a physical barrier that has developed into a physiological one for many pilots. Pilots would try to limit the amount of times they leave the cockpit. This could be for a multitude of reasons, and I cannot speak for every pilot. However, by limiting drinking fluids, there are less needs arising to visit the bathroom, and accordingly a corresponding rise in the kidney stones.

On 24th March, 2015, a mass homicide/suicide occurred on Germanwings Flight 9525 from Barcelona, Spain, to Düsseldorf, Germany. The co-pilot locked the Captain out of the cockpit and deliberately crashed the plane.

Many regulating authorities and airlines now require at least two people in the cockpit at all times whilst in flight. So the pilots have to call up a cabin crew member to come in whilst we visit the bathroom. Yes, you read that correctly, we have to ask to go to the toilet! And, of course, we always seem to need to go when the cabin crew is just about to start a service.

It adds another layer of complexity and explains why some pilots try limiting their fluids so they don't have to step outside too often.

SMOKING IN A PLANE
Thankfully, something that has pretty much been relegated to history. Smoke, fire or fumes, are things you don't want on an aircraft.

From a comfort point of view for non-smokers, it is a given that this is a better outcome. Certainly preferable to the old days of the smoking and non-smoking sections being separated by a curtain. Second-hand smoke anyone? The main reason smoking has been stopped by most airlines, is that smoldering or still-lit butts, matches etc., pose a great risk of starting a fire.

I have, at times, flown when passengers have smoked in the toilets, thinking they will get away with it. The smoke detectors are very good, as fire is just so dangerous on board an aircraft. The Cabin Crew will be alerted, and alarms sound in the flight deck. Hopefully everything (butts and matches) is accounted for and any chance of a fire has been extinguished. Then the offender will be handed over to the authorities on arrival.

WHAT IS A KNOT?
A knot is a unit of measurement used at sea and in the air. It is one nautical mile per hour. A statute mile is about 200feet longer than a nautical mile.

Its history originates from the days when mariners would measure their vessel's speed by throwing a buoyant object over the side and timing how long it took to travel from bow to stern (front of the ship to the back). This was called a Dutchman's log.

Then sailors started tying knots at uniform intervals in the rope, and to one end of the rope a piece of wood was attached. This was thrown out of the ship. As the vessel moved forward, the rope rolled out freely for a specific time frame. When the time was up, the number of knots that had gone over the ship's side was counted and used to calculate the ship's speed.

For your reference, one knot is close enough to 1mph. For my metric readers, you can double it and it will be pretty close. One knot is about 2kph

HOW DOES A JET ENGINE WORK?

When pilots are studying for their final Air Transport License theory exams, there is an entire subject devoted to the study of Gas Turbines. But I will endeavor to keep it simple.

A car engine runs on a cycle of intake (air and fuel), compression, ignition and then exhaust. Each cylinder in your car engine is doing this thousands of times per minute. A jet engine does the same thing, however, it is a constant process not a cycle.

Air comes into the engine and goes through a number of stages of a compressor, and the air is compressed many times over. This compressed air goes into the combustion chamber where it is mixed with fuel and ignited. As the fuel-air mixture burns, it expands rapidly and is exhausted out the rear of the engine via the turbine.

The turbine uses that energy to rotate the fan, which pushes the aircraft forward. This energy is also sent to the compressor at the front of the engine that keeps the process running.

WHAT DO YOU MEAN WHEN YOU SAY FINAL APPROACH?

This has possibly been heard in an announcement that a pilot or cabin crew has made. Most passengers won't have picked up on the word 'final' but the nervous flyer will have.

It has nothing to do in any way of an aircraft emergency or a non-normal landing. An aircraft has a number of phases of flight, pre-flight, take-off, climb, cruise, descent, approach, and landing. The approach phase is where the pilots begin to slow the aircraft and deploy flaps and landing gear.

Approach is also where pilots fly the aircraft using landing systems to fly through cloud (they're pretty much used all the time, even if the aircraft is not in cloud). These approaches are also broken down into initial and final approach. It has to do with standard operating procedures and speed restrictions. Yes, we have speed restrictions.

So when the phrase 'final approach' was mentioned, it was a little bit of technical jargon that has crept in. But now that you know, you will have a better understanding of which part of the flight they are referring to.

SO SPEED RESTRICTIONS EXIST...ANY SPEED CAMERAS FOR GOING TOO FAST?

No speed cameras; however, you can go too fast. As airline traffic is increasing and airports become more congested, air traffic controllers must reduce separation. Don't be concerned about getting too close to collide, when you are landing it is unlikely you will get closer than five miles (9km) to the aircraft in front of you.

This spacing allows enough time for the landing aircraft to safely slow and vacate the runway via an appropriate taxiway. So if you speed up too much, the runway may not be clear and we will not get cleared to land. This means we are required to do a go-around, which means applying power and climbing back up to a high enough altitude to come back around and try again.

A go-around can also be called a missed approach or an aborted landing. It is a perfectly normal maneuver for pilots. They are practiced every time we do re-current simulator training. They can be conducted for the above reason, not getting visual through the clouds or not being stable enough for the landing.

So all this flying stuff is safe, and now I have just told you that we may be not stable enough for landing. How does that work? An aircraft has a great deal of inertia and it must be managed in the right way to ensure a safe landing, or the ability to conduct a go-around. If we come in too fast, the aircraft will try to slow to the speed we require. Yes, we are still flying the aircraft but commanding the aircraft to fly a certain speed. Have you ever driven a car or ridden a bike down a hill? It wants to keep accelerating. An aircraft does the same thing; however, the only way an aircraft can slow is to reduce power/thrust.

We don't want the engines at idle power. If we do have to abort our landing, we need full power available quickly. We fly what is known as a stable approach. This means we have the landing flaps set, aircraft at the correct speed, and the thrust set at an appropriate level. It can be as much as 50% of full power. This way, should full power be needed, the engines can accelerate quickly from this 50%.

If we are coming in to land too fast, the engines will be at an idle power setting. Then if maximum power was required they won't spool up (accelerate) fast enough to help the aircraft climb away as it needs.

Yes, your aircraft is safe. This scenario of not being stable has unfortunately destroyed aircraft and caused fatalities in the past. But with each accident, lessons are learnt, and procedures changed to prevent re-occurrence.

When taking off, most of the time full power isn't used. It saves fuel, wear and tear on the aircraft, and reduces the noise output. When a go-around is conducted, the aircraft can use full power. It gives a real kick of power and this can surprise some people.

Case Study:
How noisy can a go-around be?

The answer can vary depending on who is on board!

I had my family on board once when I completed a go around. On this occasion, we had too much tailwind to complete a safe landing.

After we completed our actions to go-around and the aircraft started climbing away, I heard my then 4-year-old daughter squeal with excitement. Yes, heard it through the bullet proof door!

Fortunately, I have told my wife stories of go-arounds before and she explained to the passenger seated next to them what was happening... after she calmed the excited child down!

SOMETIMES IF WE ARE LATE, THE PILOTS SAY THEY WILL SPEED UP TO GET BACK ON SCHEDULE. SO WHY DON'T YOU FLY FASTER ALL THE TIME?

An aircraft is planned to fly at a certain speed to be economically viable. The faster the aircraft flies the more fuel will be used. It is a logarithmic scale. That means that if an aircraft doubles its speed, it will quadruple its fuel burn. Following on from this would be higher ticket prices for you, the passenger. When the Concorde flew across the Atlantic Ocean it was higher and faster than the regular commercial jet traffic, but you certainly paid for the privilege.

An aircraft flying through air meets air resistance, also known as drag. Imagine putting your hand out a car window at slow speed then accelerating up to freeway speed - you can feel the force of this drag. The faster the aircraft flies, the more effect this drag has on the speed of the aircraft and therefore more fuel is required by the engines to overcome this drag.

By flying faster there is more wear and tear on the aircraft, so there can be a corresponding increase in associated maintenance costs.

However, flight crew have duty limits, so there is a risk that if a flight gets delayed too much, those limits can be exceeded and the crew cannot continue. This risks the airline having to spend money on calling out new crew or accommodating passengers after a flight is cancelled. This can cost an airline over $100,000. Imagine 300 people all needing hotels, transport and meal vouchers. Then double it for all the passengers at the other end, where the plane isn't arriving.

In these scenarios the airline would prefer the pilots fly a bit faster and use more fuel. Alternatively, the aircraft could slow a little bit and the costs of the flight would reduce. It is a delicate balance in keeping the schedule on track but keeping your costs to operate the service in check.

The winds at altitude can also affect the speed at which you get to your destination. Pilots will look at all the en-route wind information when when trying to work out how to arrive at the destination quickly.

AIR ROUTES AND SHORT CUTS

The other trick pilots will look for is to obtain track shortening from Air Traffic Control. As we have no marked streets on which to fly at altitude, we fly along published routes known as airways. These airways are created for popular routes and link up waypoints. Waypoints are given 5-letter identifiers that can be pronounced. Waypoints can be hundreds of miles apart but they all have their own GPS coordinates. This allows an aircraft to store within the aircraft flight management systems a record of every waypoint and means the aircraft can navigate to any one of them. See the picture of the Sydney area below. The straight line – V169 – that is going south-west out of Sydney is an air route. The black stars underneath Sydney out over the water - DEENA and KAMPI – are waypoints.

In the earlier days of aviation, aircraft were purely navigated by radio aids and this meant remaining within range of the aid. On long over-water flights or remote-area flights, dead reckoning was used. Radio navigation aids are slowly being turned off. They cost money to upgrade and maintain, whereas GPS has a greater degree of accuracy and is, to a certain extent, free to use.

So as your aircraft travels along these air routes, pilots might see inefficient dog legs that can be cut to save time. I say 'might see,' but I am certain they will. Pilots love flying but if we can shave off some time, it feels like a little win for everyone.

Once the possible shortcut has been identified, pilots will request permission from Air Traffic Control. The controller will have to ascertain that no potential conflicts arise by granting the new tracking. If none exists, they clear us to the new waypoint and hopefully a little bit closer to our schedule.

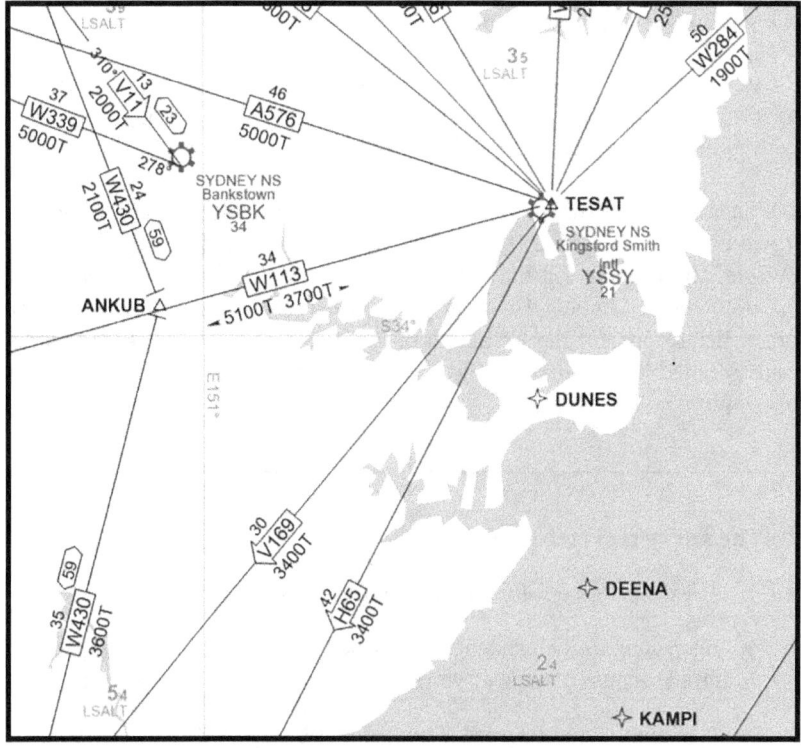

Reproduced with permission of Jeppesen Sanderson, Inc
NOT FOR NAVIGATIONAL USE
©Jeppesen Sanderson, Inc. 2018

WHAT IF MY PLANE GETS ICE ON IT?

Ice on the wings and tail can be fatal. The ice alters the smooth airflow over the wings. Smooth airflow assists in the production of lift. If ice accumulates on the wings, it distorts the smooth, laminar flow of the air over the wing and lift is reduced. If the lift is reduced too much, there is the potential of an aerodynamic stall. (I touch on what an aerodynamic stall is in chapter 6.)

Whilst the aircraft is in flight, this doesn't present as big an issue as it does on the ground. The aircraft will have anti-ice equipment on the wings and engines. These systems use electrics or hot air from the engines to heat up the leading-edge surfaces. This causes the ice to melt and fall off, or prevents its formation altogether.

Some smaller aircraft have de-icing boots. If you can see a black section on the front of your wing, this is a de-icing boot that looks like big rubber balloons. When the anti-ice is turned on, they inflate, which cracks the ice and it breaks off. If required, it can be used over and over again.

On the ground, de-icing and anti-icing operations involve a complex operation of spraying the aircraft wings and control surfaces. They are sprayed with a mixture of heated alcohol and water.

If an aircraft has been parked for a while, say overnight, and ice has formed, it will need to be de-iced. If conditions such as snow or freezing fog are still present, the aircraft will have to be anti-iced. Both procedures involve the use of the heated liquids. However, the anti-ice solution has certain chemical properties to prevent the formation of ice for a given period. This period of time is called 'holdover time' and the aircraft must take off before this time has expired.

The savvy traveler knows:

- ✈ The checklists ensure that no items are missed!

- ✈ Keep your seatbelt fastened even when the sign is off. It is repeated often because it will keep you safe in case of any unexpected bumps.

- ✈ Turbulence is just a word. Think of it as bumpy air.

- ✈ It is unlikely you will see fuel coming out of the wing. If your aircraft has an emergency and is returning at short notice, it might. But you will probably be aware of the emergency. If you do see something that looks strange, ask the Cabin Crew. They will appreciate you letting them know.

- ✈ If it is a trail of mist at the wing tip, that is water vapor.

- ✈ Out your window, can you see the street signs the pilots and ATC are using? Mostly black – that's your track. White and red means a runway.

- ✈ The autopilot is probably flying but the pilots are commanding it. They monitor and will take over if it doesn't respond the way it should.

- Pilots are very conservative. They will avoid bad weather. After all, they would be the first ones to fly through it!

- What type of aircraft are you on? Pull out the safety briefing card from the seat pocket - it will tell you.

- Pilots fly one type of aircraft at a time, so they are expert operators!

- There are multiple ways of communicating so radio failures are not a problem.

- The aircraft flight number you have is probably the call sign the pilots are using on this flight.

- Bird strikes can happen. Fortunately, you are in the bigger bird and will come out on top.

- Aircraft do get cleaned but have sanitizer wipes or gels with you.

- No, you will not get stuck on a toilet seat but please don't try to! And no, your business doesn't go into the air. The plane has a holding tank for that.

- Nobody can open a door inflight. There are special procedures to get them opened quickly in an emergency on the ground.

- Be a savvy traveler. Let the person behind you know you are reclining your seat, especially at meal times. Don't participate in air-rage or smoke on board.

- Final approach is nothing sinister. It is just part of getting ready to land.

- If the pilots can save time on the journey they will – they pedal faster!

CHAPTER 3

AFTER LANDING

WHAT IS THE DIFFERENCE BETWEEN A GOOD LANDING AND A BAD ONE?

This is very subjective. Pilots and passengers have different criteria of what constitutes the difference between the two. Passengers are generally happy with a smooth touchdown and gradual, smooth braking. In gusty winds with crosswinds and rain, pilots prefer to put the plane down a little firmer.

The reason we think this is better than a nice smooth landing is, we need to make a positive (i.e. firm) landing touchdown. This gets all the things that work in our favor to assist in stopping, working for us. It takes a great deal of energy to stop an aircraft. After touchdown, the autobrakes work, speed brakes or ground spoilers pop up, and we have reverse thrust available to us.

We want to land in the area between 1000-1500ft (300-600m) in from the runway end. All our landing-performance calculations are based on doing so. We don't want to float along the runway for a smooth landing but not have enough room to stop. There is a saying: 'one of the most useless things in aviation is runway behind you.'

Remember we are controlling a mass of anywhere from 100,000-800,000lb at 140-150mph (50,000-394,000kg at 220-240km/hr). We are also making minute corrections allowing for wind gusts and temperature thermals. We also may have been awake all night. Most landings are ok. Some are great, and the passengers love that. And sometimes they aren't so good, and we hate that, but the next one will be better.

CAN YOU CHOOSE TO FLY INTERNATIONAL OR DOMESTIC? WHAT IS THE DIFFERENCE?

This can also be referred to as long-haul versus short-haul, and really depends on the size of the aircraft you are flying.

Narrow-body aircraft are generally more suited to shorter flights - under the 4-5 hours mark. Wide-body aircraft can fly short sectors but are more capable of longer flights.

It is a complex calculation but has to do with aircraft economies of scale. The cost to carry fuel over longer distances is significant and therefore must be offset by carrying more passengers or freight.

Narrow body or wide body – how to tell the difference? Easiest way is how many aisles are there in the passenger cabin? If it is one aisle down the center of the plane, you can be certain you are on a narrow body, the most common types being A320 or B737. Alternatively, if there is a middle row of seats with two aisles either side, then sections of seats against the windows, you are on a wide body.

DO YOU FLY DOMESTIC OR INTERNATIONAL? DO YOU WANT TO FLY THE BIG ONES?

I fly internationally, with occasional domestic sectors. Some pilots don't like living out of a suitcase and want to be home every night. I love the travel and the chance to explore, shop, and eat in different locations. But each to their own.

Some pilots may not have a choice. It may be a domestic airline. As to the size of the machine you fly, often we don't have a choice – pilots fly the machines their airline operates.

So why don't you go to an airline that has the plane you want to fly? Most airlines have a seniority list. It dictates most of your life – rostering, leave requests, fleet assignments. What that means is if you are a very senior Captain in Airline A and you decide to leave for greener pastures at Airline B, you will go right to the bottom of the list – the most junior pilot. And no, not as a Captain. You would be become a Second or First Officer, depending upon the airline.

It doesn't always work like that though. If an airline experiences a period of rapid growth and expands quickly, it may need to hire ready-made Captains. There is a rigorous process to upgrade from First Officer to Captain. It is a lengthy process with lots of work involved, not just the changing of seats. The Captain sits on the left-hand side, the First Officer on the right.

By employing direct-entry Captains (i.e. those external to the seniority list), it can create friction with the pilots who are lower on the seniority list. They may feel they have waited their turn and have been overlooked for promotion.

Some airlines may also hire expats. They can become employees or contract-based pilots. Often times, these are used to plug shortfalls in training programs. They can also be for insurance purposes, whereby an insurance company requires a certain number of expatriate pilots. This often occurs

in a developing aviation market where the experience levels may be lower. It is thought that by bringing more experienced pilots into the operation, the airline becomes safer and, accordingly, insurance and lease costs get reduced for the airline.

This phenomenon is happening in China at the moment. They have/are expanding at such a rate they cannot crew all their flights with local pilots. To put this growth in perspective, in 2003 I worked at a training college in Western Australia where I was training Chinese nationals to obtain their pilot's license. That shows how well-planned China was for the explosion in aviation traffic. But it still hasn't been enough.

By employing expatriate pilots, it can create friction with the local pilots. Often the expat pilots get paid better and receive other benefits not available to local pilots. However, the money has to be high enough to attract enough pilots to live and work overseas. The local pilots would feel that the expat pilots are taking up a promotion slot that should be available to them.

It is an emotive issue and I have been fortunate not to have been affected by it, yet.

ARE YOU A CAPTAIN? A CAPTAIN HAS FOUR STRIPES. WHAT DO THE OTHER PILOTS GET CALLED AND HOW MANY STRIPES DO THEY GET?

At the moment, I am a First Officer (FO) and I have three stripes, and sometimes may be referred to as a Senior First Officer. Junior First Officers or Second Officers (SO) have two stripes. Not every airline has the JFO or SO.

The promotion from SO to FO is loosely based on time and seniority. When spots become available and you have been in the company a certain period, the option to move up is granted.

First officers have the opportunity to be promoted to Captain only when an opening becomes available. These openings go on seniority. It is often surprising to most people outside the industry that there is no merit-based promotion.

I must add this doesn't mean everybody is upgraded and it is not automatic. Each airline will have its own system of recording semi-annual performances of each pilot. Each pilot must meet the minimum performance standards or the opportunity to be promoted will not be available to them. Additionally, not every pilot will opt for promotion either. Whilst the allure of increased rank and salary is tangible, sometimes other intangibles of preferable lifestyle, schedule, destinations, take precedence.

WHAT DOES SENIORITY MEAN? IS THERE REALLY A SENIORITY LIST?

You bet there really is a list and pilots know their particular seniority number and the guys/gals in front of them. It is simply referred to as 'your number.'

In airlines with seniority lists your quality of life is determined by your number. Your number is dictated by the day you joined the airline. Your career is defined by your number. You bid your preferences for things like aircraft, type, basing, particular trips, and vacations. The success of your preferences comes down to where your number falls, both within the airline itself, your aircraft, and base. So you can see the most important thing is your number.

It is at the same time fair and frustrating. It is probably the best system available as you move up the food chain. It can be maddening when you are at the bottom of the list. Seniority is a great thing, if you are senior! When you are junior it isn't the case.

Seniority is not transferrable from one airline to another. If you change airlines, you go back to the bottom of the list and start the climb again. This includes scenarios if your carrier goes bust. In the economic downturn after the global financial crisis, there were a number of carriers that laid off or furloughed hundreds of pilots. In Australia after 9/11, the second major carrier Ansett folded leaving everybody out of work. (The corporate closure of this airline was unrelated to the 9/11 attacks, it just occurred at a similar time.) In both these scenarios, pilots who were fortunate enough to secure jobs started at the bottom again. This doesn't mean starting as a Captain again either, it is starting at the bottom rung.

Seniority can also be worked in reverse order. In times of economic contraction, Captains can become First Officers, First Officers become Second Officers or unemployed. If the number of pilots must be reduced, they work backwards from the most recently employed. Some pilots are lucky and join at the right time in a period of rapid growth and get an element of safety or buffer with plenty of pilots underneath them. Others can have a rotten run of luck and have this scenario happen several times in the space of a career.

Pilots who are laid off or furloughed will probably remain a token employee and can hopefully be re-employed once conditions improve. The seniority system will work in this case too, with the senior pilots brought back first.

CAN YOU VISIT THE COCKPIT?

This question is, in part, the catalyst for this book. When I was a kid, I loved going up for a look to see the pilots and what they were doing.

Unfortunately, since the terrorist attacks of 9/11, cockpits are now almost completely off limits. There may be the opportunity to visit the flight deck after the flight is complete.

I will always endeavor to invite kids or passengers I speak to during the flight up to the cockpit. I really enjoy the look on the faces of people who marvel at what they see. Many look at all the switches and say, "Wow!" The kids are drawn to the big displays, probably a result of being an iPad generation.

It is always a great memory for passengers (airlines might now refer to them as customers) to go up the front and get some pictures.

The problem with being at the end of the flight, is most people just want to get off the plane. Flight crew are no exception! But if the chance ever presents itself, jump at it. You can see by the picture on the front cover, the modern flight deck does look pretty spectacular. Well as far as offices go, I am pretty happy with it!

So, if you are on my flight, ask the Cabin Crew if you can visit after the flight. Most pilots will be happy to have some visitors.

WHAT ARE THE ONGOING REQUIREMENTS AND TRAINING?

Twice a year pilots undergo training and assessment sessions in a simulator over a couple of days. This is called a cyclic program, and over the course of two years, pilots will have covered most emergencies we would be reasonably expected to handle.

Each session always covers things like engine failures during take-off, aborted landings, and rejected take-offs. Each particular session has its own criteria.

We could deal with: volcanic ash, medical emergencies, pilot incapacitation, problems with aircraft hydraulics or electrics, bomb threats, and for good measure the Check Captains that can play havoc with the weather we are exposed to. The Check Captain is the person operating the simulator and providing guidance and assessment depending upon the type of event being conducted.

In the days leading up to my own simulator sessions, I tend to feel a bit anxious. I want to do well, but I just want to get it over with. It is hard to relax with a big test hanging over your head. However, it is a great relief leaving once you have completed it.

In addition to the simulator recurrent training, pilots undergo annual line checks. This happens in the aircraft on regular scheduled flights. In these assessments the checker can either be an operating crew member or they may sit in the jump seat. The flight assessment is done to observe the crew members operating the aircraft to ensure they are following the company and manufacturers procedures correctly. Recent events and issues are discussed during the cruise phase to ensure the latest knowledge is passed on to everybody.

Pilots undergo ongoing training and assessment throughout their careers. Even the people doing the checks are assessed.

Case Study:

Built a simulator but didn't like tests.

I worked with a guy who loved flying and had even built his own Boeing B737 simulator at home in his garage. He was involved in operations planning. I asked him why he didn't want to fly for a living and get paid to do it. He said he just couldn't deal with the stress of ongoing examinations. Good decision, I say.

HOW DO YOU BEAT JETLAG?

This could probably be a book in itself, and I don't necessarily have it conquered myself. There probably are as many theories as there are flights in a day. It really depends on how long you will be in your destination.

Generally flying 'west is best' as you are extending your circadian rhythm. Flying East is harder as you are trying to compress your circadian rhythm. Your circadian rhythm is basically an internal clock that is running in the background of your brain and cycles between sleepiness and alertness at regular intervals. It can also be referred to as your sleep/wake cycle.

So what does extend and compress your circadian rhythm mean? If you go to bed at 10pm it is quite easy to stay awake for another two hours if you were flying west. For the most part it is harder to go to bed earlier, say 8pm, if you were flying east.

You can try to get into the new time zone as quick as you can or if it is a short visit (often the case for aircrew) stay in your original time zone. You will probably need an alarm clock to get up after a short nap or to wake up at the new morning time. Some might say avoid alcohol, but alcohol can help you to relax. Some people say exercise, some people say nap. Some say fresh air, others say cold to sleep, warm for awake. Like I said, many theories but it really depends on your body, what you will be doing and for how long.

Case Study:

My alarm has no snooze button.

After flying all night to reach our destination, I will collapse into bed. Unfortunately, I cannot sleep too long as I have to sleep again that night before the early morning call to fly back. I have to get up, eat, exercise, and check in with the family.

My foolproof alarm will ensure I get up after about 4-5 hours of sleep. This alarm has no snooze button and wont wake anybody else up.

I would love to have had this paragraphed sponsored by Apple Watch, Fitbit or Seiko but it isn't their product that helps you get up.

This alarm is just a big drink of water. Whilst the timing isn't quite specific, it does work every time!

The savvy traveler knows:

- ✈ There is a difference between a good and bad landing. It doesn't correlate to smooth or rough touchdown.

- ✈ Often there is not a lot of choice as to which machine a pilot will fly. It depends on the airline they work for and where they are on the list.

- ✈ Can you spot the stripes of the pilots walking through the terminal? Work out the pecking order.

- ✈ Yes, you can certainly ask to visit the cockpit, but access probably won't be granted until after the flight.

CHAPTER 4

I HATE IT WHEN...

I HEAR "LADIES AND GENTLEMEN, WE HAVE A SLIGHT TECHNICAL DELAY."

Flight crew public announcements (P.A.) can be a really effective tool within the airline. However, they can also be a big liability if poorly delivered.

Firstly, P.A.s will be announced when we have a problem that is or will be impacting our departure time. Modern airliners are extremely complex machines and preventive maintenance cannot always pre-empt breakdowns.

One school of thought is that it is better to give a little information or a lot of information. Why? Well, despite airlines and aircraft coming a long way forward in terms of safety, some passengers still have a great fear of flying (I am hoping by reading this book I will allay some of those unfounded fears).

The above P.A. is preferable to saying something like we are having trouble starting an engine. Additionally, the aircraft are just so complex it may take too much time to explain.

Pilots will generally try to put ourselves in the place of the passengers. If there is sufficient time and it isn't too complex, it may be explained fully. By doing so, passengers will appreciate a limited amount of our technical language that will make them feel confident of the operation. Too much and there is a risk of scaring nervous flyers with specifics that can be misinterpreted

The manuals my airline uses for aircraft to see if we can depart is between 1000-1700 pages long, depending on which manufacturer! Look around the aircraft you are sitting on next time. We could have a problem with: air conditioning, automatic flight, communications, electrical power, equipment or aircraft furnishings, fire protection, flight controls, fuel, hydraulic power, ice/rain protection, indicating/recording systems, landing gear, lights, navigation, oxygen, pneumatics, information systems, auxiliary power units, doors, windows, engine and fuel control, ignition, air, engine instruments, exhaust/thrust reversers, oil and starting systems.

OK, you have just boarded, put your bag up, settled in and fastened your seatbelt. Let's say I now make the public announcement from the flight deck. The problem we have is one navigation light on the wing isn't working. Fortunately, we have two separate systems. We just turn on the other system and we are ok to fly. However, the bigger the aircraft, the more paperwork there is involved. We would have to radio to get an engineer to return to the aircraft to complete that paperwork so we are legal to fly.

So, it could be a simple fix as above, but a nervous flyer will imagine any number of situations – the aircraft collided with another one, was the plane hit by lightning?

Sometimes, though, the considerations will be more complex. Another issue that often occurs is the Auxiliary Power Unit (APU) isn't working. This is the little engine in the tail cone of the aircraft. It supplies electricity and air-conditioning to the aircraft on the ground. So, the aircraft will be (or get) hot and stuffy as passengers board. In this scenario, we would delay boarding until the last minute to limit the amount of uncomfortable time for passengers.

At most airports, permission for Air Traffic Control (ATC) is also required as you are starting an engine in your parking spot (normally this is done as you are pushing back, as the APU provides the air or power to start turning the engine). In this scenario, we use an air or electric cart or even bottles of pressurized air. It will require extra vigilance from ground crews to ensure nothing is sucked into the engine. The aircraft is then pushed back and stopped where we use air or electricity from the running engine to start subsequent engines. This may require increasing power on the running engine to provide enough air/electricity to get the other(s) started.

By increasing the power or thrust on the running engine, this causes the hot exhaust gases to come out the rear of the engine a lot faster. While this is all happening, we are liaising with the ground crew and ATC. The goal is to not blow anything over or prevent another aircraft from departing or arriving at their parking spot.

WE ARE JUST WAITING ON THE LAST OF THE PAPERWORK.

It is surprising airlines are moving towards a thing called less paper cockpits, but paperwork can still slow us down. Aircraft used to carry a stack of manuals on board the aircraft, so much so that when they had to be changed over, you would often see somebody wheeling them along on a little trolley. There was aircraft operating manuals that could run to thousands of pages, then airways manuals and charts that were binders about the size of two house bricks…and just as heavy.

These all added considerable weight to the aircraft. If there was a change to the manuals coming up, there would be two sets carried until the changeover date (this is because the time the manuals are due to be changed over the aircraft may be away from a home base, where they would be changed).

Carrying around all this extra weight cost money. Every take-off was at a heavier weight so more power was needed, flying heavier means the aircraft couldn't go as high or fly as efficiently. Fuel is usually the biggest expense an airline has so any chance to save it they will jump at. Also, the heavier an aircraft is, the more energy is required to stop it on landing, so the brakes suffer more wear and tear. Let's say a set of these manuals weighed 30kg. Doesn't seem like a huge amount in the overall weight. However, it you factor in that extra usage on each take off, cruise, and landing. Then each aircraft is doing several times a day, multiplied by an airline's fleet of aircraft then cost savings can be significant.

So what does this mythical paperwork consist of? It is often said, 'the bigger the aircraft the more paperwork is required.' Each airline is different and often each point of departure and arrival are different in the paperwork they require. I will touch on a few that tend to hold up the 'getting away' part of your flight.

THE AIRCRAFT'S TECHNICAL OR TECH LOG.

This is the record of everything maintenance and defect-wise related to the aircraft. It is a little bit like a car service logbook but a lot more in depth. It can cover bumps and scratches on the outside of the aircraft, maintenance that has been done or will be due soon etc. Engineers will often take the aircraft for maintenance and then release the aircraft back to service. What they have done, and what is left outstanding, is recorded. This way the pilots can see what has been done, and there is also a service record for regulating authorities. The nervous flyers will possibly quip in here that this is where accident investigators will look for clues to what went wrong. But quite often a lot of maintenance is preventative, which is working to avoid situations that caused accidents in the past.

But to some degree, yes. It is a legal document, and everything needs to be signed-off to say the aircraft is serviceable for flight. Hopefully the tech log is left on the aircraft so the pilots can have a thorough look through it whilst we wait. Then if engineers come in to make changes, these can be checked to confirm everything is ok before we get underway.

FUEL RECEIPTS AND DOCKETS.

You will often see the refueling trucks zipping around airports and wonder... do they really carry enough fuel to fill up an A380? Those fuel truck don't necessarily have fuel in them, but they pump from big underground storage tanks into the aircraft. Next time you are waiting for your flight to board, have a look to see if you can see a refueling truck hooked up to an aircraft, you may see they also have a hose connected to the ground.

Fuel orders and deliveries can be in many different weight ranges depending upon the country you are in – kilos, pounds or gallons. The flight you are on may require 30 tons of fuel. However, the aircraft arrived on its last flight with 9 ton. So you expect to receive 21 tons of fuel but the fuel receipt indicates that you actually received XX liters or gallons.

A bit of math is required to convert but I am sure there is probably an app that has been made for that. Alternatively, the table below can be used. Multiply in the direction of the arrow. Divide in the opposite direction. To convert 100 liters to kilograms; multiply 100 by 0.8 to give 80kgs. To convert 100lbs to kilograms divide 100 by 2.2 giving 45kgs.

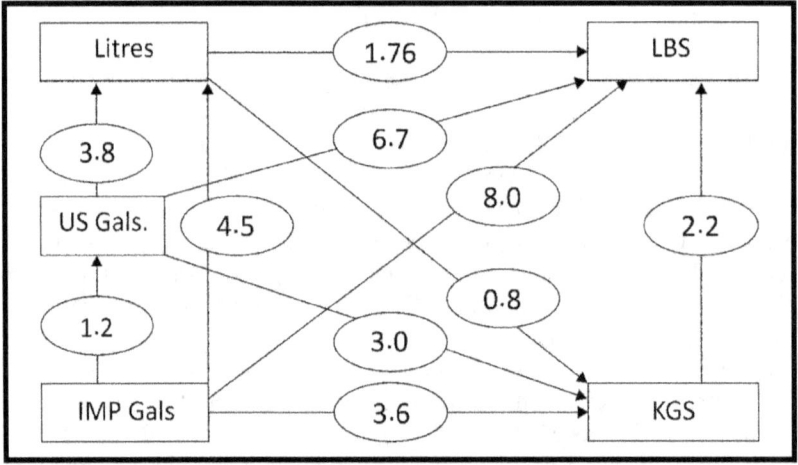

(Source: www.airservicesaustralia.com)

LOAD AND BALANCE PAPERWORK.

Imagine balancing a stick or ruler on one finger. This is a very basic description for balancing an aircraft. Your finger doesn't have to be perfectly centered for the stick to remain in place. However, there is a point that it will fall off. The difference with an aircraft is that as the aircraft flies, fuel is being burnt and the weight is not only changing but where it is distributed is also in constant flux. Depending upon the type of aircraft, fuel can be burnt from a number of different tanks and also 'moved' around by pumps during flight to ensure the aircraft stays in balance.

An aircraft has to be in balance for the entire flight. This means from when the aircraft has no fuel, also at take-off when the aircraft is heaviest, and right through to landing. That is sometimes why the Cabin Crew will ask passengers to stay in their allocated seat for take-off. Once the aircraft is airborne it is not so much of a deal if passengers move around.

Whilst the weight won't change with passengers moving around, if you move 50 passengers from the front to the rear or vice versa, the aircraft's center of gravity will also shift. If you use the finger and ruler analogy, imagine people moving forward and aft, and what this does to the ruler's balance.

This in turn can also affect the aerodynamics of the aircraft, and it will subsequently burn more or less fuel. The other more insidious danger is that aircraft control can be lost. This is unlikely with passenger movement, but it has certainly happened when freight has shifted in flight. In July 2015 a National Air Cargo Boeing 747 took off from Bagram Airfield in Afghanistan. As the aircraft rotated at take-off, some of the heavy military-vehicle cargo broke free or were not properly secured. This caused the center of gravity to rapidly move aft. Imagine all the weight on your stick moving to one side. This caused the aircraft to stall and the pilots were unable to recover, resulting in a crash and the loss of all on board. There is some spectacularly awful vision of this accident on YouTube.

Case Study:

Remain in your allocated seats until...

On one particular night flight, we were not very full in the passenger cabin. I heard the Cabin Crew make the announcement about staying in allocated seats until after departure. Once the seatbelt signs were extinguished, they were told they were free to move about the cabin.

I expected to hear that. However, I didn't expect what happened after I turned the seatbelt sign off.

One gentleman took the Cabin Crew announcement that he was free to move about the cabin, literally. He decided to upgrade himself from economy to business class.

I can't blame him for trying and had a laugh about it afterwards. For the record, he was moved back to economy and I think they altered the P.A. in future to prevent a similar reoccurrence.

Does happen!

There are some very specific procedures and computer programs to calculate all this information, and pilots must ascertain that the aircraft will remain within a center of gravity envelope. The crash mentioned above would have done this, however, the fact the freight moved was an awful accident. The airliners that you are sitting on right now have measures to prevent this occurring.

The baggage containers are locked in place to prevent them from moving. The bags may be packed in containers or loosely. If bags are stowed in the hold loosely, the compartments are separated by cargo nets. Cargo nets might not appear enough, but they will keep your suitcase firmly in place, no matter how heavy your suitcase is packed!

So the pilots will wait for paperwork regarding the load from the cargo hold – typically number of bags, amount of freight and its distribution through the aircraft. This information may be sent to a centralized loading company who will do all the calculations on specific computer programs, or the pilots may do the calculations themselves.

If the pilots do the calculations, they will also need information about the number and distribution of the passengers themselves. Why the distribution of the passengers? Well if we again go back to the analogy of the ruler on your finger... Take two passengers who both weigh 75kg. If one of those passengers is seated in row 15 (underneath your finger) and the other is in the back row (at the end of the ruler). You can imagine what that has done to the balance of your ruler.

The pilots will also be waiting on refueling paperwork as mentioned before. This permits the calculation of take-off and landing weights.

DELAYS AND THE NERVOUS FLYER
Now this information has been explained, I hope this reassures the nervous flyers out there. In reality, nothing is wrong, it is just rigorous checking that everything is correct before we go. That said, we do often have nervous flyers, who will imagine all manner of horribleness that something is in fact wrong with the plane.

This is where Cabin Crew can really earn their keep by reassuring a worried flyer that everything is ok. Pilots may also do this depending on time frame, but we are usually in a busy period just before departure. When I have gone and spoken to reassure a passenger, I just remind them that I have friends and family that want me to get home safely also. I have a vested interest in nothing going wrong on this plane. It does beg the question of future pilotless passenger aircraft.

But on this occasion, the passenger cannot be talked into staying on board. So they opt to hop off the aircraft. It does happen enough for me to mention in this book. Now because the passenger has left the aircraft, their bags must also be removed. It is a security issue to have unaccompanied bags on board. However, if it is the case of a lost/misplaced/misdirected bag being returned to its owner, then it is ok to travel without the owner being on board.

The ramp staff will probably have an idea where the bags are. It may be in a certain container that will have to be taken off, opened up and the bag found and removed. Now if the bag is in a container in the forward hold of the aircraft, all the containers in the rear will have to be removed first. It has to do with the balance of the aircraft. If the aircraft isn't unloaded in this way...well a picture tells a thousand words...

I GET TOLD EVERY TAKE-OFF AND LANDING TO STOW MY TRAY TABLE, HAVE MY SEAT BACK UPRIGHT, AND WINDOW SHADE UP.

The best way to answer this is to describe the reason why. For the number of aircraft that do have accidents more than half occur in the take-off and landing phase.

By having your tray table stowed up (or in your arm rest if you are at the pointy end of the plane) would allow you (and other passengers) to quickly exit the aircraft in the event of an emergency. Would you like to be seated in a window seat and have to fold up a couple of tray tables as you were trying to quickly escape?

The seat back upright is another similar issue. It just makes all the rows uniform and will allow a quick egress from your seat in the unlikely event of an emergency.

So the window shade is a different story. Believe me I have been tired on an overnight flight and the last thing I want to see is the sun bursting into the cabin. But it, too, has a not well-known safety-related reason. Should something abnormal occur on the take-off or landing, it can be really important to see outside to assess if there is any danger. Imagine an engine catches fire. It would be much better to know which side it was on so an evacuation can be directed the other way.

THE LIGHTS WILL BE DIMMED IN THE CABIN, IF YOU WISH TO CONTINUE READING THERE IS A LIGHT LOCATED...

Well the pilots do probably not make this announcement but when you hear a voiceover the P.A., sometimes it is hard to distinguish who is making it.

Have you ever noticed how if you are in the dark your eyes slowly become accustomed to it and you can see more than when you first entered the dark? This is in part due to the make-up of your eyes. So the brief biology lesson is that our eyes are made up of things called rods and cones. The part that sees better in the dark (rods) take a little longer to warm up. It can take up to 30 minutes for your eyes to naturally become accustomed to the lower-light conditions. Their efficiency is also affected by other conditions such as age, smoking status, etc.

So the rationale for the lights being dimmed is because you don't want to be in a brightly-lit aircraft if there is a slight chance you could end up on the outside in darkness. You won't be able to see much and with emergency services racing to the aircraft, it becomes a dangerous place. In a recent accident in San Francisco all the passengers survived the crash landing. Unfortunately, in the subsequent aircraft evacuation one person was hit and killed by an emergency vehicle. This was in daylight but possibly visibility was reduced by smoke. If an evacuation occurred at night, it would certainly add another layer of complexity to the situation.

Hence the reason Cabin Crew dims the lights. No, it isn't the pilots that do it. And just to be extra sure... make sure you eat your carrots!

The savvy traveler knows:

✈ Delays can happen for all manner of reasons. Relax. Better to be a little late in a 100% safe aircraft than to take a chance being on time in a 90% aircraft.

✈ The bigger the aircraft the bigger the volume of paperwork. Or with the increasing reliance on technology to reduce paper – the more technical glitches can happen. Ever had to reset your computer?

✈ Bags and people take time to load and unload. Don't wait for a personalized boarding call. If you are the last on board, staff may have started the offload process.

✈ Do what the Cabin Crew ask of you. They are following the rules and you will make their life easier and that will make them nicer!

CHAPTER 5

UNIFORM

I have wanted to be a pilot since before I can remember – most pilots are the same. But the first time I actually saw a pilot that I can remember was on a family vacation at Los Angeles Airport when I was about 15.

The two guys were the quintessential airline pilots and I thought they looked pretty cool having a meal at an airport restaurant. Aviator sunglasses, shiny wings, black nav bags and jackets with stripes hanging on the seat back.

HATS
Working from the top down of a pilot's uniform we should start at the hat/cap. My airline doesn't have them and I am sort of glad about that. It is another bit of uniform we would have to carry (or I am sure lose). As a former Military Officer, I have worn hats as part of a uniform and I think life is easier without one. Those pilots that do wear them only do so in the airport/hotel areas. They don't fly with them on as we wear headsets for talking on the radio.

SUNGLASSES
Shiny sunglasses. Pilots will always have sunglasses close to hand even at night or overcast days. Whilst most won't wear the big quintessential aviators there is a valid reason for having them.

On an overcast day, once you are above the clouds or on top of them, the glare from the sun reflects off them and it is quite blinding. A lot like skiing when the sun reflects off the snow. A night flight would still require sunnies close to hand as you may be doing a long flight or get delayed and dawn is never far away...especially flying east!

SHORT SLEEVES
Shirts. A sweeping generalization would be to say white or blue pilot shirts, but I have seen grey, black and green. Blue or white, looks like the clouds and sky but white is an awful color to wear when learning to fly light aircraft. So tricky just to try and keep clean.

Another thing about the shirts is they are almost always short sleeve. You can get/wear long sleeve pilot shirts but they don't quite look right. This is a sweeping generalization, but you expect a businessman to wear a long sleeve shirt and tie. If they wear a short sleeve shirt it really stands out for some reason. Same goes for pilots who wear long sleeves.

It relates back to time when pilots had to spin the propeller to get the engine started. You wouldn't want the chance your cuff could get caught on the rapidly-accelerating engine.

Another consideration is you do not want to get your shirt cuffs caught on the thrust levers. These are the levers in the center column that control power that moves the aircraft forward just like an accelerator in a car. It would not be desirable to have them brought back towards idle. The engine would still run but if it does come back to idle it can take some time to reaccelerate. This could be dangerous on the take-off roll or result in height loss up at altitude.

Back in the days of hand spinning a propeller to start the engine, pilots may have also had to complete maintenance tasks. Aircraft were a lot simpler machines back then, but also oily and grimy. It was probably preferable to wear short sleeve shirts to try and keep them clean.

Another good reason for the short shirtsleeves is the requirement for pilots to have an accurate timepiece indicating hours, minutes and seconds. Whilst this isn't a requirement on airliners, it is when a pilot is learning to fly (depending on the country and type of flight being conducted).

An aspiring airline pilot must learn to fly on instruments. This means they don't need to see outside references and can fly into cloud. During this training it is important to be able to time certain segments of the flight. Much easier to turn your wrist and have a glance at the time. The alternative could be to change hands holding the controls then flick your watch out from under the sleeve, take note of the time then change back. I am using an example of a pilot flying a light aircraft that doesn't have an autopilot. A simple example of the why things have been done and pilots are creatures of habit.

Nowadays modern airliners have timepieces built in that work off satellite and are much more accurate than a wristwatch. But I still wear a watch. I even remember to change the time zone most times! Changing time zones so often it is sometimes handy to have two time zones on your watch. Either for keeping track of time back at home or for flight planning purposes.

EPAULETTES

The bars on the shoulders. A Captain has four on each shoulder, a First Officer has three. Not all airlines have them, but Second Officers have two stripes. They are generally gold or silver on a dark background.

How come sometimes there can be two Captains flying together? Would they ever make a mistake and not roster a Captain? The Captain sits in the left-hand seat. Sometimes another Captain may occupy the right-hand seat where the First Officer normally sits. Second Officers are used for in-flight crew relief and don't occupy the controls seats for take-off or landing. The airline might be short of crew and a Captain can fill the void or the Captain in the left seat may be doing some recurrent or ongoing training.

There are always two pilots and additional crew are not always carried. It depends on the length of flight.

And in case you are wondering, no, they won't ever forget to roster a Captain on a flight!

TIES

In front of the passengers the pilots have their ties on. Many pilots take them off as soon as they reach the cockpit and out of view of the public. Personally, I don't, as I know I would most certainly forget to put it back on! But if it is really hot and we don't have air-conditioning available I might.

What you might not realize about these ties is that they aren't always 'tied.' Often the ties will be either clipped on or attached with Velcro somewhere. The rationale behind this is twofold. Again, similar to the short sleeves reasons, you would not want to have a tie get caught in a rotating propeller. So it can be quickly taken off or if it does get caught it will be removed.

Unfortunately, the other reason ties need to be removed quickly is so they cannot be used to choke aircrew (pilots and cabin crew). Since 9/11 so much has changed with regard to security. Pilots now work behind bulletproof doors but in the 1960-80s, commercial airliner hijacking was a regular occurrence. A removable tie was one of the counter-measures employed then to try and keep crew safer.

WINGS

Personally, the bit of my uniform I am the proudest about is my wings. Pilots have worked hard to earn their wings and must keep working hard to keep them. To the passengers on board or in the airport, it identifies us as the operators up the front in the cockpit. To each pilot, it symbolizes often years of hard work and study and often thousands of hours of flying experience.

Most pilots will have a collection of wings from previous training institutions and employers. I am a bit of a hoarder, so I still have all of mine. They tell a story and each set reminds me of different times in my life/career. You may occasionally see a pilot without their wings. I cannot explain that. It took me too long and I worked too hard not to wear them each time I put on my uniform.

'NAV' BAGS

Those magical black (99% of the time they are black) bags. What is in them, as they look big and heavy? Going back a while they certainly were, as pilots carried paper charts and maps. In order to save weight, a great number of airlines have or are trying to go to paperless cockpits. Now most things are done on tablet-type devices, whether in-built into the aircraft or stand-alone iPads.

Some crew may carry their personal logbook to fill out upon completion of their flight. Pilots log, amongst other things: the aircraft type, aircraft registration, other crew, route and most importantly, the flight time in a book (also been overtaken by technology) each flight they do. That's why the back cover of this book says I have a specific number of flying hours. We log each flight and tally it up as we go. It was always viewed as a badge of how experienced or how long you have been around.

Early on in my airline career I carried my own headset to use. I was young and enthusiastic but the novelty of carrying more stuff and plugging in and unplugging at the end of a shift wore me down. Much easier to use the aircraft-supplied headset and wipe it down with a sanitizing wipe.

So they are the big items that took up a great deal of space but what to fill them with now is pilot preference. I carry a jumper – the front of the aircraft can get cold soaked as it is -85/-65C outside. Also in the middle of the night when you are meant to be sleeping, your body temperature drops, so I feel cold.

I also have a bag of chargers. I am an Australian but the aircraft I fly has American power outlets and we may be flying to a third country that has a different plug again. Three plugs and then various cables for different devices.

The savvy traveler knows:

✈ Watch your crew walk through the terminal. Do they fit the description I told you? Hats, sunglasses, short sleeves, wings and the secret black bags?

Case Study:
Are you a doctor?

As we often go from one climate-controlled environment to another (hotel to transport to airport) we are not out in the elements for long.

However, on one particularly cold winter morning I had driven home and had worn my long black jacket as the short drive home wasn't long enough for the car heater to warm up sufficiently.

There was an elderly lady walking along the sidewalk next to where I had parked my car. I smiled and said good morning then I retrieved my black 'nav' bag from the trunk. She inhaled quickly and double-backed towards me.

In broken English, she queried, "Do you do house calls?" Having been awake all night, my mind was on falling into bed and I didn't hear (or listen to) her correctly. I replied "Yes, this is my house." She wanted confirmation, "You are doctor?" We both chuckled when I displayed my uniform under my jacket.

She obviously grew up in a time when home visits by the doctor were the norm and she was hoping she found one who still carried out the practice. It is the only time I have been mistaken for something other than a pilot! It was the black bag that did it.

If she only knew I hate the sight of blood and wouldn't make a very good doctor!

CHAPTER 6

WHAT CAN I SEE?

THERE ARE DIFFERENT TYPES AND COLORED LIGHTS ON THE AIRCRAFT. WHAT DO THEY ALL MEAN?

Navigation (Nav) lights: These are just like a ship at sea, so you can work out an aircraft's perspective. We always have them turned on and the green light on the right-hand side shows from directly ahead to about 135 degrees around, or 45 degrees beyond the right wing. This is where a picture will tell a thousand words. There is also a white light that shows the tail of the aircraft.

If you can see a green and a red light at the same time, that aircraft is flying directly towards you. You do see this occasionally; however, we have the third dimension of altitude so it may be flying towards you but you will (should) be at different altitudes.

How do you remember which is which? Just like a sailor would talk about the 'red port left' in the bottle. Red is the port side in nautical terms.

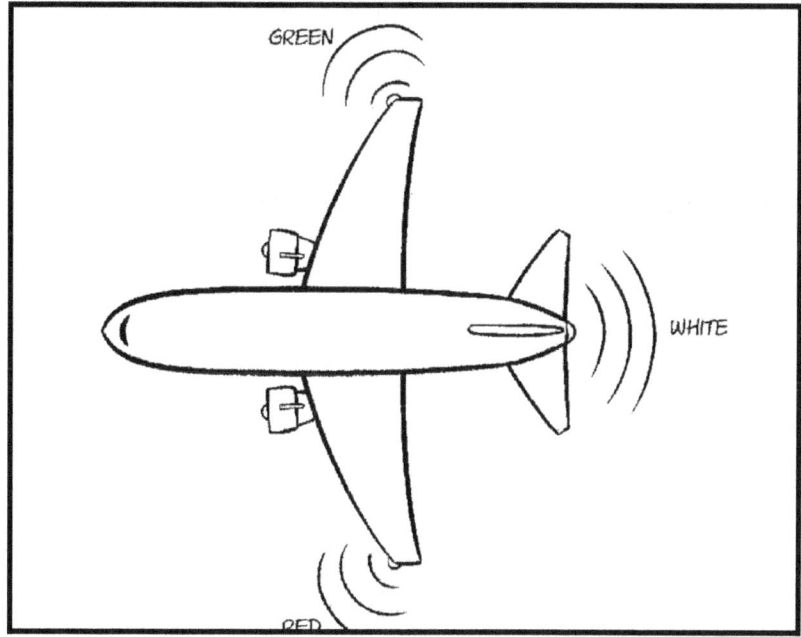

Rotating beacon(s): This is the next light that gets turned on (often there are two – one upper and one lower beacon, but controlled by the one switch).

This is turned on just prior to engines starting or the aircraft being towed. Obviously, this is a dangerous time to be walking or driving past, so it is a red flashing light that means 'stay well clear.' It is possible to be sucked into the engine inlet at the front, and the exhaust gases at the rear of the engine will be over 900F/500C degrees.

The beacon will be extinguished after the engines are turned off and spun down. The engines keep rotating for a short time afterwards and have been known to suck things – including people – in.

If it is night time, the logo lights are switched on. These are bright lights that are directed towards the airline's tail logo. I think it is more about advertising but also assists other pilots and air traffic controllers to identify aircraft. These lights are generally on the top surface of the horizontal stabilizer (the little wing at the rear of the aircraft) aiming upwards. Mostly they get turned off once we are away from the airport as nobody will be close enough (we hope) to read the tail anyway

Anti-collision lights: These are bright, white flashing lights that are usually on the wingtips and used night and day. They are turned on just prior to take-off and turned off again after the landing roll is complete and the aircraft is off the runway. Pretty much means we are in flight or about to be. Can also be found on the upper or lower fuselage.

Landing lights: These are the bright white lights you see when an aircraft is landing or taking off. They are most commonly set in the wing or associated with the nose-gear strut. Some airlines have a procedure that they are not turned on until the aircraft has been cleared for take-off or landing. This can be done as a reminder that the aircraft has been cleared to take-off or land. Might seem strange but it can assist when you are impaired by jet lag and fatigue.

Taxi lights: Used like headlights on a car so pilots can see where they are going. Usually turned on just before the aircraft moves under its own power, i.e. not being pushed back by a tug. They are white and found on the nose-wheel strut. Usually on for the take-off and landing as well.

Runway turnoff lights: If these lights are installed, they are similar to taxi lights but are aimed slightly outward of the aircraft center. This permits pilots to see where the turn markings on runways and taxiways are.

I THINK A FOUR-ENGINE PLANE IS BETTER THAN A TWO-ENGINE PLANE. IS THERE ANY DIFFERENCE BETWEEN THE TWO APART FROM FUEL BURN?

Airlines will generally prefer to operate twin-engine aircraft due to the significant difference on fuel burn. However, twin-engine aircraft must remain within 60 minutes flying time on one engine from a suitable airport.

So how does a twin-engine aircraft fly across the world's oceans or north pole? All twin-engine aircraft have an Extended Twin Engine Operations (ETOPS) certification. This extends the range to which a two-engine aircraft can fly from an emergency airport. A larger ETOPS rating means the aircraft can fly more direct routes and be further away from these other airports.

A larger ETOPS time gives the airline an advantage when routes fly long over-water or isolated routes. For example, the four-engine Airbus A380 can fly across the Pacific Ocean, direct between the West Coast of the United States and the East Coast of Australia. Let's say the two-engine Boeing 787 has an ETOPS rating of 180 minutes (it is actually much longer). This would mean the B787 would have to remain within 3 hours of its planned emergency airports. This might mean the aircraft has to dogleg a flight plan to achieve this. This could negate the benefit of flying a two versus four-engine aircraft.

Should the ETOPS certification for the B787 be increased to 300 minutes. It now only has to remain within 5 hours flying time of its planned emergency airports. Now this route will approximately be the same as the A380. So, the benefit of less fuel burn of the two-engine aircraft becomes apparent. Although, it isn't without other associated costs for ETOPS. There are more maintenance inspections and routine tasks that add costs, but as mentioned previously, fuel is usually an airline's biggest expense so it is still a cost-saving to the airline.

One of the newest aircraft in production is the Airbus A350, which has an ETOPS rating of 370 minutes. So, the manufacturer says this aircraft is safe to fly on one engine for a little over 6 hours. If it was flying on one engine at around 420kts (750km/hr) that equates to over 4,500km or 2,500nm. This theoretically means the A350 can fly anywhere in the world as there is no place on Earth that is that far away from a suitable airport.

Why theoretically? Well there are a number of other considerations. It may be able to fly to any airport; however, the airport must be available for use. There are other considerations such as weather, NOTAMs, is the airport restricted by curfew or works that would preclude a landing? All of this information is digested by the pilots in our pre-flight planning and preparation.

SO COULD A PASSENGER BE TALKED THROUGH TO SUCCESSFULLY LAND A PLANE?

In Hollywood, sure. In reality, it's a bit more complex.

Let's say you are on your modern airliner and for some reason both pilots become incapacitated. For your information, we do practice one pilot becoming incapacitated in training sessions.

Your first issue will be gaining access to the flight deck. Then it will require a Herculean amount of strength to grab one of the pilots. I would go for the lightest looking pilot – probably the First Officer. They don't say captain's physique for no reason! But you will probably be assisted by other, concerned passengers or cabin crew.

Next you are going to have to work out how to 'speak' to someone. This will involve working the VHF radios most of the time. However, more methods of communication include HF radio or more modern satellite communications.

Then you will have to explain your issue to the air traffic controllers. They will then have to get a qualified pilot or instructor to talk you through activating the automatic landing system. If that happens then yes, you would probably walk away from a safe landing, then you can just wait for Hollywood to contact you about a movie deal!

Automatic landing systems are designed so aircraft can land in conditions of poor visibility. They can also be used in good weather for practice or training.

If there wasn't anybody with any flying experience it would prove a little harder to do but not impossible. In the television show *Mythbusters*, two of the hosts without any flying training were able to land an aircraft simulator under instruction.

That said, there isn't any record of a successful 'talk-me-through-it' landing of a large jet airliner. But there have been occasions of light aircraft being talked down when the pilot became incapacitated. Who knows, maybe by reading this book you increased your chances!

HOW DOES A PLANE ACTUALLY FLY?

This is one of the first lessons pilots go through when we learn to fly. For the benefit of my valued readers, I will keep it simple. It is quite easy to get too technical and proceed down a very theory-orientated aerodynamics lesson. I have a 500-page aerodynamic text book in front of me filled with complex formulas.

It is written by a highly-qualified engineer who is certainly smarter than me. However, I can translate the information into simple-to-understand concepts so you, too, can understand how the 200-ton aircraft you are in seemingly defies the law of gravity.

Most of the time air is invisible. If you pass through fog, mist, or dust it can be 'seen.' This makes the concepts hard to imagine when comparing to, say, a ship or boat.

You can visualize the bow piercing through the water and creating a bow wave and the wash that trails astern as the vessel passes through the water. (I can't help it – Navy background showing through!) An aircraft flying through the air creates the same areas of pressure and disturbance; they are just infinitely harder to see.

Have you ever been in a car with the window down and stuck your arm outside? By merely moving the angle of your hand you alter the pressure distribution and the way your hand moves relative to the airflow. That is basically how an aircraft works.

Developing this idea further, let's consider two physics principles. Don't worry, I will keep it simple and there is no test at the end. But you will feel clever when you look out the window on your next flight and explain to your travelling companions a few aerodynamic theories.

The first item is air pressure. Total Air Pressure is made up of Static and Dynamic Pressure. Static is stationary pressure and dynamic is moving pressure. Today let's say the pressure is 10 units. If you have your hand out your car window whilst you are stopped at the traffic lights, the static pressure is 10. Dynamic is zero as you are not moving. As the car moves, the dynamic pressure starts to rise, so the static pressure must reduce.

The second physics principle is Bernoulli's theorem. This states that if there is an increase in kinetic (dynamic or moving) energy due to the increase in velocity (speed), this will be accompanied by a corresponding decrease in static pressure.

A wing has a curved upper surface, so let's imagine two air parcels – A and B. 'A' will travel above the wing and 'B' will travel below the wing. Our two air parcels will start and finish flying over the wing at the same time. As the upper surface is curved, it is longer and 'A' must travel faster than 'B' to meet up again at the end of the wing. Using Bernoulli's theorem, we now have lower pressure on the upper surface and higher underneath. This causes the wing to either lift or get sucked up depending on your school of thought but perfectly sufficient for the depth of this book.

This basic aerodynamic principle is manipulated in three planes to control the aircraft. We have pitch, yaw, and roll controlled by the elevators, rudders, and ailerons respectively.

At the rear of the aircraft there is another horizontal wing called the tail plane or elevator. The pilot can manipulate the movement of this wing by moving their controls forward and aft. This has an effect of altering the curvature of the tail plane and the forces acting upon it. These forces cause the aircraft nose to pitch up and down around the lateral axis through the center of gravity. Pilots often say if you pull back on the controls, the houses get smaller (i.e. the aircraft nose goes up), and if you push forward the houses get bigger (i.e. the nose goes down).

The next plane of motion is yaw, which is the left to right motion of the aircraft nose. The control for this is also at the rear of the aircraft but in this case, it is the vertical part of the tail. This is called the vertical stabilizer or rudder and is controlled by the rudder pedals at the pilots' feet. This force acts through the center of gravity around the vertical axis.

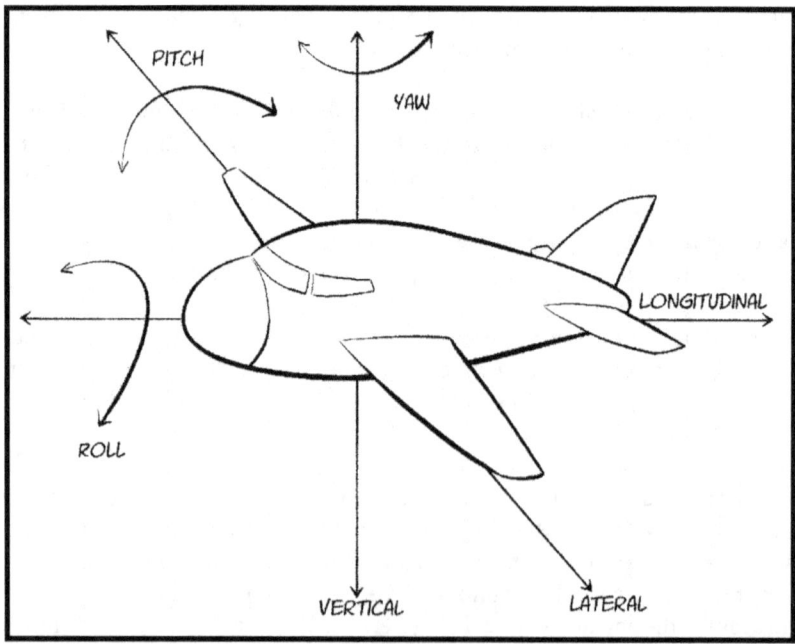

Finally, if you have a window seat you may see at the far end of the wings movable surfaces called ailerons. They cause the aircraft to roll around the lateral access through the center of gravity. The ailerons on the left and right wing work in opposite directions to one another, forcing one wing up and the other down.

There are other forces and secondary effects that come into play with flight controls. Aerodynamics is a complex subject, but you now basically understand how every aircraft gets airborne and stays aloft.

WHAT IS A STALL?

Most people relate an aircraft stall to that which can occur in a car. The jerky lurch to a stop as the engine quits running. Whilst an aircraft engine can stall, it is unlikely. It is also starting to get beyond the realms of keeping this book simple, as I would need to discuss jet engine theory beforehand. Suffice it to say, if you ever hear stall in an aviation context it is more likely an aerodynamic stall that is being discussed.

In the earlier explanation about how the aircraft flew, I discussed the two air particles A and B, flying above and below the wing respectively. Obviously, the airflow around the wing is constant and not limited to two individual particles. As our wing flies it is disturbing the air and the extent to which this is done is dependent upon the angle at which the wing presents to the relative airflow. This is known as the angle of attack.

The higher the wing presents the more airflow that is disturbed over the top of the wing. The resultant airflow is now disturbed as opposed to streamlined and the production of lift decreases. The important word there is decreases not ceases. Basically, you can stall an aircraft and still 'fly'; however, there are other issues and it is certainly not the most efficient way to fly!

CAN WE GLIDE?

Absolutely. Every aircraft can glide, some better than others. All that is required to keep flying is to ensure airflow over the wing. Obviously having some form of forward propulsion like engines is better.

If, in the unlikely event you did loose both engines, the aircraft will still fly and buy the pilots time to try and start them. How long will you continue to fly? To give an example, if you were cruising at 35,000 feet and both engines failed, you would probably glide for 10-15 minutes. Depending upon the aircraft weight and phase of flight, most airliners cruise at altitudes above this.

WHY DO YOU TAKE OFF INTO WIND?

This deals with two different speed concepts: airspeed (speed through the air) and groundspeed (speed over the ground).

For example, we need to reach an airspeed of 150kts to take off. If we are facing into a 25kt headwind, we already have an airspeed of 25kts, i.e. we have 25kts worth of airflow over the wings already assisting us to create lift. So, by the time we are travelling with a groundspeed of 125kts we are taking off.

If we took off with a 25kt tailwind, we have an airspeed of -25kts, i.e. we have -25kts of airflow over the wings but in the wrong direction. We would need to be travelling at 175kts over the ground to reach our 150kts through the air. Going fast would use up more fuel, more runway, and require more power to take off. This means ticket prices would go up.

The savvy traveler knows:

- Flashing red lights means the aircraft is being towed or the engines are about to start.

- Flashing white lights means the aircraft is on an active runway.

- Steady red and green lights show you a particular aspect (left or right side) of the aircraft. How do you remember? Green and right both have 5 letters!

- Twin-engine aircraft are just as safe as the four-engine machines.

- In an emergency, maybe you could be talked down safely but probably more in the realm of Hollywood than real life.

- Put your hand outside a moving car (not too far though) to mimic the effects of how the aircraft wing flies.

- A stall has nothing to do with the engines and relating to an automobile stall. This is the breaking up of the smooth airflow over the top off the wing.

- In the unlikely event all the engines stopped. Yes, absolutely the plane can glide.

- Taking off and landing into wind increases the air speed over the wing and, accordingly, we can take off and land at slower ground speeds.

CHAPTER 7

AIRCRAFT EQUIPMENT

Stuff you don't know about or don't want to know about.

Aircraft have a few pieces of special equipment that passengers don't often get to see. In fact, they may even be unaware that this gear is on board as they are mostly for emergency situations. Now that I have pointed them out, you may see them on your next flight, but hopefully not the first two....and no, a parachute isn't on the list!

HANDCUFFS/FLEXICUFFS
'Passenger restraint kit' is the term used for handcuffs. Generally made of strong plastic, sort of like big cable ties but could also be made of metal. These are most certainly carried. Why? Well, air rage is, unfortunately, on the rise and there can also be people with mental health issues who can have problems onboard. In order to protect the safety of the many, people who carry out or threaten violence must be restrained.

SKY MARSHALS
This is great to have on your aircraft, but you really don't want to see them. If you do, you are in a possibly very dangerous situation. They have been around since the 1960s; however, only 33 were on active service when 9/11 occurred. President Bush sought to rapidly increase their profile and numbers. Other countries have followed suit.

They are there to take over should a terrorist situation develop. They will have guns on them but will only respond in a dire circumstance. That means they will not assist with a drunk or obnoxious passenger. In this case it is difficult to understand the position the Marshal would be in. However, it is done to counter a ruse that may be employed by a terrorist seeking to ascertain if a Marshal was on board.

They, for the most part, try to remain incognito. Depending on individual organization policies, they would get involved in a life-threatening situation and only when the cabin crew have exhausted abilities to handle the situation.

The Sky Marshals don't travel on every flight. They work closely with intelligence organizations and are placed on flights with the greatest risk of hijack. If you fly with the Israeli national carrier El Al, you can be almost certain they have an equivalent service on board.

AXE OR CRASH AXE

Aircraft above a certain size are required to carry a crash axe. It is intended for prying open panels to view/fight a fire. It can also be utilized in a survival situation. With the tragedy of German Wings Flight 9525, there were reports the Captain tried to break into the cockpit with the axe after his suicidal co-pilot locked him out. I am sure the Captain would have tried everything at his disposal to get in, but the axe is stored in the flight deck.

FIRE EXTINGUISHERS

Fire extinguishers are another item you don't want to see utilized on your flight but they're required for firefighting on commercial aircraft. You may see them scattered throughout the aircraft and also located in the galleys and flight deck.

The most common type use Halon. Halon is a liquefied, compressed gas that stops the spread of fire by chemically disrupting combustion. The benefit of Halon is that it can be used on all classes or types of fire. A water fire extinguisher is no good for an electrical fire, but Halon can hopefully extinguish them all!

The cargo holds and engines also house their own integral fire-suppression systems. These are activated by the pilots, or in some instances, automatically.

CREW REST COMPARTMENTS

Airline pilots and cabin crew have rest and duty times. Trust me, you don't want a tired crew either trying to land a plane or get you out of your aircraft in the event of an emergency.

The crew rest compartments are found on most long-haul aircraft. They can generally be accessed via a hidden stairwell as they are either up in the roof or underneath the main cabin.

Each airline has its own setup, but generally speaking there is somewhere to sit and somewhere to sleep. To those outside the industry it makes us look like we don't work very hard if we have a bed at work. However, fatigue is a very real issue. Granted, in cruise the alert levels are lower; however, on descent and approach to land, your crew are probably working very hard.

Australia has a very robust road safety campaign about not driving tired as that is when mistakes occur. If someone has been awake for over 18 hours, it is said their performance can be impaired to a level similar to somebody with a blood alcohol level of .05% (that is the legal driving limit in Australia). So it is much safer to supply the crew with proper rest and sleeping facilities so they are 100% ready for landing.

Pilots often have a separate compartment from the cabin crew. Does anybody join the mile-high club whilst there? I doubt it very much as when it is your break, you just want to sleep. I am sure it has happened though.

DEFIBRILLATOR

It's not required medical equipment; however, many airlines now carry defibrillators on board. There have been instances where passengers have been saved by their use and, unfortunately, cases where they may have saved passengers, but the devices were not carried. Some types of defibrillators have been designed so untrained people can employ them in an emergency with simple easy to use, illustrated and audio instructions.

All cabin crew and most pilots are trained to use them. The refresher training is conducted annually on a day called Emergency Procedures (EPs is the shorthand lingo). That said, the defibrillators now carried on some aircraft are designed so that anybody can use them. The parts are clearly numbered or named so the 'pads' can be placed on the correct body parts. Unlike the movies there is no rubbing together of the pads and a doctor saying 'stand clear.' But there is an automated voice that will tell you to stand back as the shock is about to be given. What happens next? Hopefully the patient recovers. I haven't seen it used for a real emergency, and I hope you don't have to either but it is good knowing that it is there.

PORTABLE OXYGEN

Another piece of equipment that is used regularly for ill passengers is the portable oxygen bottles. When I say regularly I would guess maybe one in every ten flights it is used. People can be feeling poorly for any number of reasons and supplemental oxygen can greatly assist people to feel better. With the increased altitude of the cabin and a reduced amount of oxygen available, people can sometimes have difficulty breathing. There are still also nervous flyers around and I sincerely hope if you are one of them, that by reading this book I allay your fears. The oxygen can sometimes merely have a placebo effect but certainly helps to reassure passengers.

The cabin crew can administer this if they think it is needed or somebody requests it. The bottle looks like a small scuba diving tank and has a lightweight plastic cord and mask. Crew would then periodically check on the passenger to make sure their condition is improving.

If for some reason they don't improve the issue would be elevated to the next level of seeking out a trained medical professional. It always amazes me whenever I have had a medical issue on board, just how often there is someone who fits that requirement. I have had flights with doctors on board, but also have been lucky enough (or the passengers they were treating were too) to have had great nurses, paramedics, dentists, surgeons and people who have done more advanced first aid training who have stepped in to help.

SURVEILLANCE CAMERAS

Despite not having visitors to the flight deck, there will be times crew come and go. We have toilet breaks, rest breaks, paperwork, meals, and sometimes face-to-face communication is needed between the crew. The crew member wishing to gain entry calls up the flight deck and we can answer but before we grant access, we look on the cameras to firstly make sure they are a crew member (Emirates has thousands of cabin crew, so it would be impossible to remember all the names). Secondly, we are also ensuring they are not under duress by a would-be hijacker attempting to gain entry. Only when all is deemed safe, would we open the door.

Some airlines have security departments that monitor these feeds continually via a live stream from the aircraft.

Some of the larger aircraft such as the Airbus A380 and Boeing 777 have additional cameras externally. These are used to assist the pilots taxing in airport terminal areas. On a Qantas A380 you can use the inflight entertainment to view one of the cameras mounted in the tail of the aircraft that looks down over the top of the plane. There isn't much to see in the cruise phase of flight but cool to watch the take-off and landing parts of the flight.

I have also been asked if the cameras let us view inside the bathroom. That answer is no. We can tell from our system pages or indicators on the flight deck if the bathroom is occupied but no there is no camera in the bathroom.

GRAB HANDLES

Did you see them as you boarded your last flight? Chances are you may have. They are located at each door/emergency exit. They are about shoulder height and whilst they are good for holding on to whilst having a chat, their location, should give you a clue as to their use.

In the event of an emergency evacuation, the crew would hold on to these and assist in getting everyone out quickly. If there was nothing like this to hold onto, there is every chance that the crew member at that particular door could be inadvertently pushed out in the hysteria to escape.

COCKPIT CAMERA

Some air safety regulators around the world have recently been campaigning for cockpit video cameras. These cameras would record what happens on a flight deck and supplement the cockpit voice recorder and the flight data recorder. These are often referred to as the black boxes air crash investigators look for in the event of a crash. They can help piece together what happened for the investigators. Despite the name, they are usually a fluorescent color to help them stand out.

There has been quite a push back from pilots about this. Personally, I can see the possible use, but it doesn't really provide any more information that the voice and flight data recorders don't. We know and understand the need to record the other information, but this could be used in other less palatable ways. Would you like to have your every move recorded by your boss? It isn't that pilots are doing anything wrong but there is such a thing as personal privacy. The voice recorder and data recorder covers everything that is required.

The savvy traveler knows:

- There is some interesting unseen equipment on board. Most you don't really want to see as it means there is something unpleasant occurring.

- That said, it is nice to know it is there and available for security, first aid, or firefighting.

- If you are near the entry to the flight deck door, there is every chance you will appear on the flight deck cameras.

- As you enter or depart your aircraft, see if you can spot the emergency grab handles...whilst you say a friendly hello or goodbye to your cabin crew.

CHAPTER 8

MISCELLANEOUS

FUTURE TECHNOLOGY

In an earlier section I describe how many airlines have gone, or are starting to go, paperless. This, in part, is being aided by the rapid advances in technology and tablets gaining widespread acceptance in everyday life.

By having documents electronically there are literally thousands of pages of manuals not being carried in hard copy. This adds up to a significant weight reduction and a corresponding reduction in fuel burn. If you calculate that for each sector and aircraft, and multiply it over the airlines' fleets, the cost savings are significant.

These tablets are now commonplace from airliners down to light aircraft. However, like anything new, this has given rise to fresh safety-related issues. There have been cases of pilots relying solely on their device with no plans for back-up. This is hoping that the tablet performs without issue and that the data being used is approved and updated in a timely manner.

There is an abundance of software applications running into several hundred on any of the equivalent app stores. That said, there is only about half a dozen approved to provide the required information. There are unapproved applications, and a sole reliance on these would be foolhardy.

Fortunately, airliners have a rigorous change management process to ensure this doesn't happen. They also have stand-alone backups. This can entail a separate device, condensed hard-copy manuals, or the B787 has an electronic library on board with all the manuals.

WILL WE SEE PILOTLESS AIRCRAFT?

From my employment prospect perspective, I hope not any time soon. But then again, maybe logging on to a computer from the living room to fly would avoid the less desirable traits of flying – jet lag, sitting down for long periods, and most importantly, airline food!

However, this would entail massive safety and technological advances. It is not insurmountable, but the huge financial implication will also require consideration. Airport infrastructure and air traffic control systems would have to be redeveloped. How will aircraft receive instructions and carry them out on the ground and in the air?

There is an obsession with technology and that 'there is an app for that' mentality. We think computers can do everything better than us. To an extent they are great aids to what we do. I have often heard the comparison of a highly-qualified surgeon who uses technology to improve diagnoses and treatment. In a similar way we do that with technology in the flight deck.

(Author's note: I am in no way comparing the years of hard graft a surgeon does to complete their training to that of a pilot, I am merely comparing the tools we use.)

With the advent and rise in popularity of remotely-controlled drones, it is easy to imagine a future airliner without a pilot. But drones have different tasks. You can't just make it bigger and put in some seats and away you go.

Pilotless vehicles have also been demonstrated to operate successful test flights. However, a few test flights don't prove the long-term viability of mass transport in widespread use.

Ah, so now I sound like an aviator who can't envisage a world in which his livelihood has disappeared like a television repair man or Morse code operator.

We are seeing the development of driverless cars, trucks, and trains, and people will believe the aircraft should be next. The thing with these vehicles is, they are operating in a two-dimensional airspace and if something goes wrong, they can pull over or just stop. That doesn't work at 35,000 feet! The pilots are more like systems managers telling the aircraft how it needs to be flown.

There is also false assumption that the removal of humans removes the possibility of human error. Complex computer systems already control most of the aircraft systems, with pilots spending long periods monitoring. This advanced technology has greatly assisted in making aviation safer. Whilst automation has made pilots' workload more manageable, the aircraft is still under the control of a human. This makes the world's crowded skies safer. The paradox here is technology has also threatened lives at various times.

Planes are now extremely safe and easy to fly. When failures occur they are now presenting situations to pilots that are extremely confusing and potentially beyond the realms of being recoverable. An Air France jet crashed after incorrect speed data was displayed. The autopilot disconnected, and this surprised the pilots and they reacted to false information. In an eerie scenario another aircraft gave warnings of flying at the maximum and minimum speeds at the same time. It then rapidly pitched down injuring a number of crew and passengers.

These two events stand out a challenge to the assumption that technology is fail-safe and is superior to pilots' abilities. The problem herein is that the technology is also designed by humans. All the lines of computer code and algorithms that go into designing aircraft automation are not fail-safe. People will always make mistakes, that is why it is called 'human error'; however, you need to be able to override these computer system commands and take back control.

The thing with computers is they are processors that are really great at following code. So things that have very defined procedures for completing tasks, yes they can be computerized. Much of what pilots do in a day-to-day setting involves following standard operating procedures (SOPs). So yes, those things can certainly be codified and operated by a computer, just like the autopilots do now. Certainly, the routine things could be automated, hence autopilot assist by doing the flying straight and level segments, which is mundane. What the computers cannot do however, is be flexible or think for themselves.

What about all those accidents that happen when they blame 'pilot error?' Yes, it has happened before where the pilots were at fault, but this isn't always the case. You never see the times where pilots have avoided an incident or accident.

An often-highlighted event of recent years is the miracle on the Hudson. Captain Chesley Sullenberger successfully ditched the aircraft on the Hudson river in New York. Ditching is landing on the water. His aircraft flew through a flock of geese and suffered a dual engine failure. This took piloting skill to manually fly the aircraft and make rapid decisions in the short space of 204 seconds from take-off to eventual ditching in the river. What would a pilotless aircraft have done in this case? The engines were no good, it required human skill to guide the aircraft down.

It can be easy to throw the pilots under the bus when it comes to blame for human error. However, all those computer programs that assist in flying the aircraft are also written by humans and are certainly not infallible.

Technology improves rapidly and is becoming commonplace in our homes and workplaces. Often times, the human has become the weak link. However, it must be remembered that sometimes the human is the strongest link.

PILOT ERROR

You may have heard of pilot error causing an outcome. What you will never hear of, though, is pilot actions that avoid negative outcomes. It could be through experience and pilot actions that accidents and incidents are avoided.

Flying takes place in a very dynamic environment. It is always changing with weather and Air Traffic Control demands, and this gives rise to a need for decision-making. It is constant and requires continual re-evaluation. Has the right decision been made? What is the next decision?

Why won't you hear about it? It is our job. But more importantly, we as pilots love what we do and would never put anyone's life in jeopardy. We are sons, daughters, wives, husbands, parents, just like you. We have taken years of hard work to achieve our roles and we want to get home safely too.

Over time and with experience, pilots sometimes have a gut feel when things may not be right. On each flight we bring with us all the experience we have accumulated over the thousands of hours and many miles we have flown.

So, for now, pilots still have control over that automation.

WHAT HAPPENED TO MALAYSIAN AIRLINES MH370?

If I had a dollar for each time I had been asked about this, I would be rich!

I think every pilot has a theory but really wouldn't like sharing it unless in the company of other pilots.

Nobody knows what happened, and pilots are loathe to speculate. We know that speculation could come back to haunt us down the track and we would certainly appreciate the benefit of the doubt. Unfortunately, mud sticks. Rumors of the 'Playboy Pilot' and the Captain with his own simulator at home do little to help the cause of finding the aircraft or providing closure to the victims' families.

The wild theories abound from hijacking, murderous love triangles, suicide, theft, and aircraft malfunction. Each new theory has its five minutes of headlines before the next revelation. Should these revelations in the fullness of time be shown to be disproven, there will be no headline grabbing apology, it will be just on to the next sensation. And right or wrong, the crew of MH370 will have no right of reply.

Adding to the confusion is the availability of experts willing to speak to the media. Accident investigations use hundreds of people, certifiable experts and thousands of man-hours to conclude investigations. Often these self-proclaimed experts have their own agendas to push and have merely cobbled together some facts from less than reliable sources to proclaim the outcome.

An aviation expert these days is merely a click away.

IN LIGHT OF AN ACCIDENT

Aviation is a peculiar profession. Most pilots will look up and watch planes and go to airshows on our days off. You could say that we love it to death, but the peculiar part is that if we meet our ends in the line of work, it's most likely that we will receive the blame.

There is blame long before any proof is found.

There will be blame by the media and surviving passengers will upload video and camera pictures to the Internet. It is a by-product to the digital age we live in. Those pictures will be shared around the world, maybe even before survivors have been rescued. Is there a benefit to the likes, shares, and OMG comments? It is doubtful. But aircraft accidents are headline-makers and the more shares only highlights its sensational nature.

The rescue and recovery operations take second place whilst grandiose assumptions are offered by all and sundry. No facts are present and only voyeurs are satiated.

Family members are prevented from being informed with respect and dignity about the loss of loved ones. Families of the crew will be subjected to the consequences or even the speculation of the actions carried out. Still no facts are present.

Data and voice recorders will be located and analyzed and maybe after lengthy investigations, it will be found that it isn't the pilots' fault.

WHO IS THE SAFEST/BEST AIRLINE?

So, is the airline I am about to fly on safe? If they aren't the safest, who is? Who isn't? And many other versions of such are often posed to pilots, and are impossible to answer. It is a futile exercise to work out.

As I have discussed in other parts of this book, crashes are extremely rare occurrences. When they do occur, lessons are learnt and passed on to all other operators. Safety audits are conducted all the time. You could go crazy trying to compare which airline is safer. There are millions of flights every year and an infinitesimal percentage of crashing.

WHAT ABOUT LOW-COST CARRIERS? ARE THEY STILL SAFE?

A low-cost carrier or LCC still has the same expense overheads for wages, fuel, maintenance etc. The low-cost bit comes in by charging you a bare-bones ticket price (i.e. low cost) but then making money in a user-pays system. No bags, no problems. Want to take bags, they will charge you. Don't want food or drink on board, ok. Each individual element is broken down and the end user (passenger) pays.

There are way too many rules, check and safety implications for an airline to bypass safety in order to save money. The implications for failing a safety audit are severe. Airlines can be grounded with notices to show cause as to why they should continue to operate, and in some cases they can be banned from flying into certain country's airspace.

IS A BOEING SAFER THAN AN AIRBUS?

Take your best guess. Commercial aircraft are safe by any valid meaning. That said, pilots will always have a favorite aircraft.

Which one is it?

It is always the one we are flying at the moment!

CAN GIRLS/FEMALES/WOMEN BECOME PILOTS?

If there is a young girl reading this and wondering, can I? I will tell you absolutely, you can! There is a big push to get more women into aviation.

In the company I work for, we actually have a number of pilots who are father and daughter. They have all had the fantastic opportunity to fly together, too. My little girl says she wants to be a pilot. I think it is because she says, "Daddy does holidays for work." I can't argue with her logic, but I would certainly foster any ambition she has to undertake the role.

There are certainly more avenues for females to become pilots. Depending on the country, the military has been open to female pilots for some time. There are also groups and forums about getting women into aviation and aerospace.

I will be honest, I received some blunt feedback about designing the cover of this book from a female pilot. She stressed to me that all references in this book make out that all pilots are males. On the back cover you will see it says, 'what do the pilots mean when they say...' Previously it said, 'when he says.' I saw the error of my ways. So thanks, Davida!

It wasn't intentional; I was just in a typing frenzy and relating it to myself. So hopefully, this does inspire a young lady to take up flying. If it does, please let me know. I would love to hear your story.

The savvy traveler knows:

✈ Technology aids the profession and does make it safer.

✈ Trust me, you want somebody up the front with just as much invested as you in getting to your destination safely.

✈ Pilot error can happen but that is why there is at least two pilots. We use standard operating procedures and use checklists to minimize the chances of these errors leading to something undesired.

✈ I think everybody who has ever flown hopes they do find MH370, to give closure to the families and answer the unanswered.

✈ There is no best aircraft or airline. Pilots have a soft spot for the one they are flying currently.

✈ Just about anybody can become a pilot. The effort and expense is huge, but you truly can be paid to stare out the window!

✈ But what you really wanted to know all along is...

CHAPTER 9

THE TWO MOST POPULAR QUESTIONS

HOW MUCH MONEY DO YOU EARN?

You know why the jumbo jet deck has that big hump? It is because the pilots are sitting on really fat wallets! Haha, I wish.

I will never forget when I was doing my ATPL (Air Transport Pilot License) exams and my instructor Pete 'Sparse' Griffiths would always wheel out that joke. This period of time was not really much fun – cramming for exams and preparing for increasingly difficult flights.

This instructor was great at seeing the look of angst on our faces after wrestling with a practice exam question for 30 minutes and getting it wrong. He would throw his comment in and tell us to "stick with it" as the rewards would be worth it.

Just about every pilot I have come across has had some sort of setback in their flying career. Most have stuck with it and the reward is doing a job that many people envy.

The financial rewards vary. They vary from airline to airline, country to country, and your rank.

I will give you another perspective. I spent around $80,000USD ($150,000AUD) on my qualifications before I started with an airline. I hope that all pilots will be rewarded commensurate with the investment they have made in their training and ongoing requirements and responsibilities they undertake every time they go to work.

DO YOU GET FREE FLIGHTS?

No. Discounted yes, but free? No. Well not unless you count the airline positioning me to another location to operate a flight or send me home.

As to the discounted flights, most airline employees receive them, but they come with a catch. Whilst the flights are quite to very cheap, you are on standby or sub-load. This means you can get offloaded for full-fare paying passengers or freight. Alternatively, you may just not get on the flight at all.

Each airline has its own pecking order for who gets on first. It could be related to your level/position in the company, or it could be when you purchased the ticket.

It is great to get cheap flights; however, I find it quite a stressful process. You are constantly looking to see how many free seats there are and whether you will get on. If you have a booking for accommodation or the more pressing need to return to work, it can add another layer of stress.

Case Study:
Cheaper versus confirmed.

I was leaving my house in Singapore and there were 10 seats left on the flight to Kuala Lumpur I hoped to board.

In the 20 minutes it took to get a taxi to the airport and check in, those seats had been sold. I had visions of going back home while my non-refundable accommodation remained empty.

Fortunately, there were some no shows and we got on the flight. Was it worth saving the money? Sitting in Kuala Lumpur I think so, but if I had to go back home, no way.

IN CONCLUSION

Ladies and gentlemen, good evening once again from the flight deck. We have almost concluded our journey. You are not too far away from your destination and finishing this book.

Congratulations on reading this and coming a long way to be considered a savvy traveler. As more and more people take to the skies for work and leisure, many will have no understanding of what is really going on. Feel free to impart your knowledge.

Ladies and gentlemen, boys and girls, thank you for taking this journey with me. It has been a pleasure having you along and I hope to see you on board soon.

INTERVIEWS

Interview with Customer Service Manager 'Kickem off', Claire Sutherland

What is your role?

As a Customer Service Manager, I am responsible to the Pilot in Command (PIC) for the supervision of the cabin crew and the administration of the in-cabin service. I will liaise with the pilots to ensure proper management of the cabin crew and to minimize the impact of any operational requirements; for example, weather, PAs, early descents, diversions on the cabin service.

How long have you flown?

I have been flying for 11 years so far.

What is your favorite destination?

Honolulu is absolutely my favorite. The shopping and the weather. It is a nice way to break away from winter occasionally and the shopping. Oh, gee, the shopping is great!

How often do you go into the flight deck?

I will visit at the beginning of the flight where we will exchange information with the pilots. I will let them know if we have any special requirements for arrival such as passenger with mobility issue and a general feel of the cabin. Are people happy, tired, or any rowdy passengers. During this time the pilots will let me know our expected time of arrival and when we are likely to start a descent. This allows me time to plan service and crew rest breaks.

After that I will contact the pilots every so often to see if they need any food, drinks, or bathroom breaks. This will depend on the time of day or night, and what the cabin crew workload is like. I will contact them before we start a service so any requests can be accomplished before we start to get busy. Alternatively, they may contact me to ask the same.

Do you get many requests to visit 'behind the flight deck door?' What would you say to somebody who asked?

Since the 9/11 hijackings, the cockpit has become an isolated place. Back in the good old days, you could visit in flight. The pilots appreciated having somebody visit to talk about the profession and demonstrate what they were doing.

I get a lot of children asking to go up and see the flight deck. Most of the time it will really depend on the pilots, and I have a pretty good idea of whether they will grant the opportunity to do so. Sometimes they can be undergoing training or checking themselves and it may add a bit too much unwanted pressure. Or sometimes, the pilots themselves are waiting for the last of the passengers to leave as they will be racing to catch a flight themselves.

Adults sometimes do and occasionally you have a real enthusiast who fill out logbooks on when they fly. They write down things like flight numbers, registration, crew names and may even ask the Captain to sign it for them.

It is a real shame as now really the only time we can accommodate visitors is after landing. Before the flight departs we are probably too busy and we need to concentrate on what we are doing and minimizing distractions is the key. If we had a very nervous flyer, one of the pilots may go out to say a quick hello and put a face to the voice. If they speak to passengers in this situation, they simply reassure them, that they too have family and friends that they want to see again and wouldn't let anything prevent that.

The nickname given to you by the author; do you really kick lots of people off?

No. Not unless it is warranted. It just happened to stick with Brett and he is really the only one who uses it.

Interview with young passengers, Adrian and Jadyn

How old are you both?

We are 13 and 11.

Where have you flown before?

We are lucky we have flown to several places. In no particular order: Fiji, Bali, Honolulu, Los Angeles, Las Vegas, Gold Coast, Cairns, Sydney, and Singapore.

Seems that you or your parents like flying to warmer places. What is your favorite destination?

We both really liked Los Angeles, because of all of the amusement parks and shopping.

I know you have both gone behind the flight deck door for a look. Tell us about the time you visited the cockpit after your flight? Where were you going? What did you like? What did you ask? Did anything surprise you?

It was one of our first flights and some time ago on our return home after Fiji. It was really interesting, and we couldn't get over how many buttons and lights there was. We asked lots of questions about what each thing did and how the pilots actually fly. Mum and Dad took some great photos too!

Interview with a nervous flyer, Sarah

Can you please tell us a little bit about why you were afraid/nervous to fly?

I don't like the feeling of not being in control or there being so many unknowns. I also have this overwhelming irrational feeling that if something bad is going to happen on a plane i.e extreme turbulence, birds hitting the engine, it's going to be on a plane that I am on. All part of being someone who can suffer from anxiety.

How do you feel now, having read the book?

Having really no knowledge of how a plane works this book has answered so many questions that previously have led to many uneasy thoughts. It was really great to actually get an insight into how a plane works and what happens when certain things occur. The next time I board a plane it will be with a bit more confidence. A really interesting read for all, thanks Brett.

What would you say is the best bit about flying?

The adventure waiting at the other end, it's a little bit of discomfort for a great reward at the end.

Your favourite destination?

Lennox Head, New South Wales, on the East Coast of Australia.

What would you say to somebody who is nervous to fly?

Reading this book will help! Try to look at it as a time to shut off and relax. The pilots and crew are so well trained in just about every scenario that you're in the best hands you'd want to be in while flying to your destination.

Interview with the Senior Check Captain (Assessor)

What does your role involve?
My job is to carry out proficiency checks and training of our pilots on behalf of the regulator. I will also liaise with the Standards Manager on matters relating to training/checking and providing advice, as required.

How long have you flown?
A long time! Several decades. If I said anymore, people might start hinting I need to retire!

Are you fair or formidable in your assessments?
In my job I do have to enforce standards, the limits of which are clearly described. Unfortunately, sometimes not everybody is at his or her best and checks can be failed. Most pilots are their own harshest critics and will know how they have fared. I hope to set a friendly, professional environment that is conducive to pilots performing at their best on the day.

Why do pilots not seem to relish going into the simulator sessions?
Pilots go through simulator cyclic training/assessment twice a year. There are so many scenarios that must be studied and prepared for and the crews want to perform at their best. It is assessed, and pilots genuinely care and want to do well. It is just like going for an exam for your license every 6 months!

So it is a good thing then?
Sure is. If they come out of the session having learned something and gained confidence in their process and procedures it is a positive outcome for all concerned.

Favorite destination?
I love all the places I fly-travel to, but just like Dorothy in the *Wizard of Oz*, 'there is no place like home!'

GLOSSARY

Aborted landing – also known as a go-around. Pilots apply full power to go back up into the air and go back around for another attempt at landing. Can occur for many reasons; e.g. aircraft is too fast, safety cars on the runway, previous aircraft hits a bird, previous aircraft still on the runway. A normal flight maneuver for pilots but can be unexpected by passengers.

ATC – Air Traffic Control. The people who organize and guide all the planes in the air and on the ground.

Bank – to roll an aircraft around its longitudinal axis (an imaginary line running from nose to tail). Applying bank to an aircraft turns it.

Check Captain (Checkie) – a Captain who performs assessment on other crew members in simulators and in aircraft on behalf of the company and regulating authorities.

Cockpit – where the pilots sit and control the aircraft.

CPDLC – Controller Pilot Data Link Communications. This allows pilots and Air Traffic Control to communicate to one another by what is essentially text message. This is used primarily in remote/over-water areas where VHF coverage may be limited.

CSM/CM – Customer Service Manager/Cabin Manager. Can also be called Chief Purser. The Captain is in charge of the aircraft, the CSM is in charge of the cabin and all the crew and passengers in it.

Drag – that resistance force of the air as the plane flies through it.

EPs – Emergency Procedures. This is training undergone by pilots and cabin crew annually to ensure they are proficient at carrying out emergency responses and drills. Covers things like fires, evacuations, equipment use and limitations, sliding down the emergency escape slides, operating life rafts, and first aid. Is slightly different for cabin crew and pilots but a great deal is the same.

ETA – Estimated Time of Arrival.

ETD – Estimated Time of Departure.

ETOPS – stands for Extend-Range Twin-Engine Operational Performance Standard. The short answer is long-range flights on planes with two engines.

FO – First Officer. The second-in-command on the flight, and the pilot who sits on the right-hand side.

Fuselage – the body of the plane that is shaped like a tube. Does not include the wings, tail, or under carriage.

Glide/Glider – a plane without an engine. All planes can glide, they just differ greatly in how well they glide.

HF – High Frequency. Long range radio communications. If you imagine a really old radio with static, that is what it sounds like. Used predominately for remote-area communications.

Jump seat(s) – these are the seats in the flight deck that are not occupied by the operating (Captain and First Officer) crew.

Lift – the aerodynamic force that pushes the aircraft up.

PIC – Pilot-in-Command. The Captain. Sometimes there can be flights with two Captains, one will always be designated as the pilot-in-command.

Radar – Radio Detection and Ranging. A device that sends out a radio pulse. If it bounces back, a calculation is completed to ascertain the distance away the object is. Used by pilots in the aircraft to avoid bad weather. Also used by Air Traffic Control to monitor aircraft tracking.

Rejected take-off – when something abnormal occurs on the take-off roll, before a special calculated speed (V1), pilots will reject the take off. V1 is calculated every take-off and it is runway, aircraft weight, and weather dependent.

Thrust – the force of forward propulsion provided by a propeller or jet engine.

Under carriage – the wheels, brakes, and struts that hold them all together.

VHF – Very High Frequency. This is the type of radio that pilots use the most to talk to Air Traffic Control (and other aircraft or the airline staff at a particular base). To be in range it works on line-of-sight. So the higher an aircraft is, the better the range. Once your aircraft is beyond the range of that particular antenna, a frequency change will be required or switching to a different means of communication such as HF or CPDLC.

WITH THANKS

I didn't get to where I am on my own. Like an aircraft departing on a flight, there are many people who have provided support, advice, accommodation, or finances over my journey.

Firstly, to all the passengers who have kept me employed – thank you.

To my parents and grandparents who were backers from the beginning, also known as financiers because aviation is an expensive habit to maintain. Kirsty and Amara, for the events I have missed or when I have been a jetlagged, tired, and grumpy person to be around – thanks for understanding.

To the family and friends who were brave enough to come on a flight in a light aircraft when I was building my hours and experience. DJ and Craig, my first passengers. Lucy and Rob, I am sure my flights were more fun than any business class trips you have since completed! Paul and Pete, I take credit for inspiring you to take flight for overseas destinations. Pete for organizing my work experience and my first foray into the world of aviation. Scotty, I think of you like a brother and I look up to all you have done flying-wise.

Writing some sections really choked me up. Miss you Kyser and all you did for Team Alpha Floor.

Julie Postance for all the meetings at the library, advice and homework tasks you set to ensure I got this book off the ground!

David, Karen and Amy, for supporting me on my early first steps into this career and showing faith in me when I needed it most.

Darren Howie from Vortex Aviation Photography (www.vortexaviationphotography.com.au) for providing the awesome images you see on the cover of this book.

Paul Cox (www.paulcoxillustration.com) for the great images drawn from my loose descriptions.

Thanks to my marvelous editor, Amanda Spedding, the amount of assistance you gave was amazing.

To those that helped me in the designing and publishing by voting on the cover, proofreading, doing interviews and providing the testimonials; AJ, Brent, Chen Quiling, Chris, Claire, Davida, Dirk, DJ, Gav, George, Jadyn, Jess, Jo, Liao Wei, Nisha, Paul, Peng Xiang, Rachel, Sarah, Sally, Shayne, Steady, Tony. Thank you so much.

To all the crews I have flown with, I have enjoyed the ride and learnt something from each and every one of you, and I hope I have been an enjoyable crew member to fly with.

Jess, thanks for relighting the spark in me to finish this book.

Thank you, to all the people I have come across who have asked these questions, that gave me the impetus to actually create this.

Thanks for reading.

Brett

www.ingramcontent.com/pod-product-compliance
Lightning Source LLC
Chambersburg PA
CBHW072051290426
44110CB00014B/1630